Praise for

the next
TEN minutes

"Like yoga for your mind, Andrew Peterson's simple but profound thought experiments may just change your life. I'll be practicing these mental calisthenics for a long time to come."

—**Jessica Berger Gross**, author of *enLIGHTened*

"A spoonful of humor—and a few simple exercises—help the wisdom go down, and Andrew Peterson uses an expert hand and gentle humor to remind us that every moment offers the potential for transformation."

—**Meredith Maran**, author of *My Lie*

"The Next Ten Minutes is a substantial yet simple antidote to our usual pulsating and mind-numbing twenty-first-century lives."

—**John Sommers-Flanagan, PhD**, author of *Becoming an Ethical Helping Professional*

the next
TEN minutes

51 Absurdly Simple Ways to Seize the Moment

Andrew Peterson, EdD

ATRIA BOOKS
New York London Toronto Sydney

BEYOND WORDS
Hillsboro, Oregon

ATRIA BOOKS
A Division of Simon & Schuster, Inc.
1230 Avenue of the Americas
New York, NY 10020

BEYOND WORDS
20827 N.W. Cornell Road, Suite 500
Hillsboro, Oregon 97124-9808
503-531-8700 / 503-531-8773 fax
www.beyondword.com

Copyright © 2010 Andrew Peterson

All rights reserved, including the right to reproduce this book or portions thereof in any form whatsoever without the prior written permission of Atria Books/Beyond Words Publishing, Inc., except where permitted by law.

Managing editor: Lindsay S. Brown
Copyeditor: Jade Chan
Design: Devon Smith
Composition: William H. Brunson Typography Services

First Atria Books/Beyond Words hardcover edition October 2010

ATRIA BOOKS and colophon are trademarks of Simon & Schuster, Inc.
Beyond Words Publishing is a division of Simon & Schuster, Inc.

For more information about special discounts for bulk purchases, please contact Simon & Schuster Special Sales at 1-866-506-1949 or business@simonandschuster.com.

The Simon & Schuster Speakers Bureau can bring authors to your live event. For more information or to book an event, contact the Simon & Schuster Speakers Bureau at 1-866-248-3049 or visit our website at www.simonspeakers.com.

Manufactured in the United States of America

10 9 8 7 6 5 4 3 2 1

Library of Congress Cataloging-in-Publication Data

Peterson, Andrew (Andrew L.)
    The next ten minutes : 51 absurdly simple ways to seize the moment / Andrew Peterson.
        p.   cm.
    Includes bibliographical references.
        1. Self-actualization (Psychology).   2. Change (Psychology).
    3. Mind and body.   4. Self-help techniques.   I. Title.
    BF637.S4P4477   2010
    158.1—dc22

                                                            2010018321

ISBN: 978-1-58270-274-2
ISBN: 978-1-4391-9523-9 (ebook)

The corporate mission of Beyond Words Publishing, Inc.: *Inspire to Integrity*

Contents

Introduction

My Daily Meditation Practice
Or, How Failing to Meditate Taught Me How to Meditate

Every morning I meditate for ten minutes.

That's right. I do.

After all, it's just ten minutes out of my day. And I always feel better afterward. In fact, I've noticed how the entire rest of my day goes better if I've just taken those few minutes to meditate in the morning. And I'm familiar with the research documenting the mental and physical health benefits of meditation. I should be, after all. As a psychotherapist, I am constantly encouraging my own patients to start a simple meditation practice because I know from personal experience how much it can help.

So, yeah. Every morning before I start work, I take a few minutes to meditate.

Yup.

That's what I tell myself.

If only it were true.

Okay, so I intend to meditate every day. But often I simply don't do it. I spend time thinking about it. I imagine

myself sitting in meditation. I give myself pep talks and remind myself of all the reasons meditation is good for me.

Then I check my email. Or I do a crossword puzzle.

It's puzzled me for a long time. Why do I struggle so much to get myself to do something so simple and pleasant, something that is guaranteed to improve my day?

As I finally got myself to sit down and start meditating one morning, this question was in the back of my mind. I began, like I always do, with a body scan, bringing awareness to each part of my body. Then I settled into the simple task of watching my breathing. *In, out. In, out.* Next, as inevitably happens, my mind started wandering. "I'm so glad I'm doing this," I thought. I noticed myself having this thought, and I directed my attention back to my breathing. *In, out.* Then another thought came into my mind: "If only I could make myself remember the way this feels, then I'd definitely do it every day." I noticed myself thinking that thought, and I tried to bring my focus back to my breathing again. But the thought was more powerful than my intention, and it propelled me forward into other thoughts. What is the difference, I wondered, between my state of mind when I'm trying to motivate myself to meditate and my state of mind while I'm meditating?

It occurred to me that in order to understand what propelled me from contemplation into action, I had to understand the gap that lay between those two states. So I began to focus my attention there. What did that gap have to tell me? I tracked back through my experience, isolating the moment just before I had sat down to meditate. "My mind was just blank," I thought at first. But as I moved more deeply into the memory of that moment, I realized that *blank* was the wrong word. In that moment my mind had grown still; it had emptied out. A blank mind is numb. But an empty mind is dynamic—loose and fluid, filled with possibility.

The message the gap had for me was this: Your behavior tends to be static, but your state of mind is fluid. You move rigidly and discretely from one behavior to the next, but your state of mind is constantly changing. It's extraordinarily malleable, capable of radical transformation between one moment and the next.

I realized then that I'd been going about solving my problem in the wrong way. I'd been telling myself that the issue was my "behavior," that I needed to do something differently. But that wasn't it at all. What really changed between those two moments was my state of mind. A change in behavior was the result, not the cause.

And it hit me. In this, as in so many other aspects of my life, I try to change myself by forcing myself to do things differently. That's to say, I try to change my behavior by forcing my behavior to change. It's kind of like trying

to teach a dog to sit by repeatedly forcing it into a sitting position. You can *make* a dog sit that way, but all the dog learns is how to be made to sit.

The real question, I realized, was this: how do you make a dog *want* to sit?

The answer was clear: you've got to start by changing its mind.

And that's what this book is about.

Wrong Side of the Bed

So many of my patients come to me reporting that they find themselves stuck in unproductive routines, wanting to change but unable to make themselves do so. They're looking to me for help in changing their behaviors.

But the only way I can do this is by helping them change their minds.

Sometimes this disorients people.

For instance, I was recently working with a young man who was depressed and complained about a lack of motivation. In our first session, he described to me how he would go to bed every night with the intention of waking up early and going to the gym to work out. He'd tried all sorts of things to get himself to do this. But every morning when the alarm rang, he'd feel a heavy sense of fatigue and hopelessness. He'd hit the snooze button and go back to sleep.

This was a seemingly simple problem. But as he described it, it was clear that it was filling him with despair.

I told him, "You need to do something different."

He gave me a look that said, in essence, "Well, duh."

I asked him to walk me through the experience of a typical morning, starting from the moment he awoke. As he started to talk, I interrupted him with requests for more and more detail. What position was he in when the alarm rang? How far was the clock from his bed? What was the precise moment when he could say he was aware of being awake? What was the exact sequence of thoughts from that moment forward? What could he smell? What did he hear?

He looked at me like I was crazy. But he kept answering my questions.

Once we had established the series of events in excruciating detail, I asked him another question: "What could you do differently?"

He started by repeating the things that he'd always told himself: "I can get to bed earlier. I can just force myself out of bed when the alarm rings."

I interrupted him again. "You're jumping to the conclusion," I said. "Keep it really simple. Don't try to come up with the solution; just think about something that could be different, whether or not it would actually help."

He struggled with this.

"What if you were sleeping on the other side of the bed?" I asked.

"I guess I could," he said.

"Keep going," I said. "What else could you do differently?"

He got into the spirit of things and came up with a few simple, slightly absurd ideas. He could get himself into a yoga pose the minute the alarm went off. He could have a staring contest with his cat.

"How about your thoughts?" I asked him. "What could you do differently with those?"

He considered this. "Could I think different thoughts?" he asked.

"I don't know," I said. "What do you think?"

I sent him away with instructions to pick one simple thing that he could do differently each morning. I told him not to make any particular effort to actually get out of bed, but just to do something differently and notice everything he could about the experience.

When he came in the next week, he reported that he'd been feeling a little lighter. He started telling me about a new relationship he was considering and about some problems at work. He looked different, although it was hard to put my finger on what had changed.

After a while I asked him about his morning routine.

"Oh, I knew there was something I was supposed to be doing," he said. "But actually I haven't really been thinking about it."

"That's okay," I said. "But still, I'm interested ... how have your mornings been going?"

"They're fine," he said, seeming a little irritated by my question. "But I really want to focus on this girl I was telling you about."

It was certainly a positive sign that the energy had gone out of his earlier complaint, that he was focusing on future possibilities. But he didn't seem to recognize that his chief complaint a week ago was no longer bothering him. So I pushed a bit further.

"I'm just curious," I said. "Before we move on, what was it like when you woke up on the morning after our last session?"

He thought for a moment, and a puzzled expression crossed his face.

"Actually," he said, "it was really annoying. I went to sleep on the other side of the bed, like you'd suggested. When the alarm went off, I was back on my usual side. I woke up and I just lay there, thinking about things. I really wanted to go back to sleep, but my mind was so awake that I couldn't."

Your mind was awake, I thought. That phrase told me that we were on the right track.

We went on with the session. And he went on with his life. Over time it became clear that, for a variety of reasons, a number of things in his life were changing for the better. During one session he described how he'd had an argument with his parents that usually would have put him in a bad mood for days, but this time it rolled off his back and he'd felt fine afterward. Another time, he talked about how he'd been invited to go out with some hard-drinking buddies. Usually he talked himself into agreeing to these invitations, telling himself that he would have a good time getting drunk; then he'd regret the decision soon afterward. This time he simply didn't feel the temptation, and he shrugged off the pressure that they put on him.

He didn't return on his own to the subject of getting out of bed in the morning. When I brought it up again, weeks later, he told me that it just felt "different." It didn't feel like such a big deal. Sometimes he was able to get up early, sometimes he slept in.

"I don't worry about it so much," he said.

"So what do you think has changed?" I asked, "because even though you might be doing exactly the same thing . . . it feels different."

"I guess I'm thinking about it differently."

"It seems that way," I said. "But keep going, because what you're talking about is your capacity to change how you think about your own experience. And if you can harness that ability, you can apply it to all sorts of other problems."

"It's like ..." He looked up at the ceiling, struggling to find words for his experience. "I feel like there's a part of my brain that's watching the rest of my brain."

"And how does that change things?"

"I get to decide for myself what my attitude is going to be?"

"Yeah," I said. "That's exactly it."

"Toward everything," he added.

He paused for a long moment then, considering the magnitude of the statement he'd just made.

"How is this different from how things used to be?" I asked.

"Usually I guess my brain was just sort of on automatic pilot. I'd just kind of go along. Something bad happened and I felt bad. Something good happened and I felt good. I didn't think about whether I had any choice in the matter."

"And you now know that you *do* have a choice," I said. "It will take practice to keep yourself aware of this. But you always have that choice."

I could see a question forming in his mind then.

"All this happened because I tried sleeping on the other side of the bed?"

"I think that all this happened," I said, "because you allowed the wise, observing part of your brain to take the lead for a few minutes. When you allow that to happen— even when the issue itself seems sort of silly—you change your state of mind. You become more fully aware of your own experience in the present moment. And when you do that, you open up the possibility for all sorts of change in your life."

As If

This book is dedicated to two propositions:

First: Big changes in our lives start with small shifts in our state of mind. It's not always easy to see the link between something as seemingly insignificant as sleeping on the wrong side of the bed and something as transformative as overcoming depression. But the connection is there. It's the butterfly effect operating within our own psychological development. The flap of a butterfly's wing in your state of mind can eventually set off a storm of change in your overall mental health.

Second: The seeds of change are embedded within the most ordinary activities of daily life. The mechanics of daily life are to this book what breathing is to mindfulness meditation. Because our daily routines are repetitive by their very nature, we tend to think of them as metaphors for stagnation—the "daily grind." But when we bring our full attention to the activities of daily life, we discover that activities as simple as making a list or drinking a glass of water can produce nuanced and infinitely variable experiences. And when we step back and observe our own awareness of that variability, daily life can become an act of meditation. Each of the exercises in this book is designed to help you make a small but significant shift in your state of mind, in the next ten minutes, using activities that are so utterly mundane and straightforward that you ordinarily do them without awareness.

Go into a different room.

Throw something away.

Stare at the wall.

These don't seem to be meaningful activities. We certainly don't need someone to instruct us on how to procrastinate or to breathe. But when we engage in such tasks mindfully, the routines of our daily life can be transformed.

The guiding principle behind this book is thus both true and absurd: doing routine activities *as if* they require instructions alters our state of mind. It brings us into an awareness of ourselves in the present moment. And behaving mindfully in the present moment transforms our experience.

While the benefits are profound, there's no great mystery to these exercises. These are not the lost secrets of some cloistered Tibetan monk. In fact, when I describe

these exercises to others, they often get animated and describe for me a moment in their life when they did exactly what I am describing. Often that moment was in childhood.

This has in fact been a rule of thumb for me as I created these exercises. I know that I'm on the right track when I can easily imagine a young child spontaneously doing what I am describing, just because it's interesting.

Remember this: There was a moment when we did every ordinary thing for the first time. We did it with full awareness and even with a sense of wonder. But, of course, we didn't continue doing things this way. Learned activities morphed into habitual routines. We forgot how much power our minds have to make such activities interesting. We stopped giving our brains the credit they deserve.

It is my great hope that this book will help you remember how smart your brain really is.

My Restless Mind

I have a restless mind.

Some people might call it hyperactive.

Whatever you call it, the bottom line is that I can't stand not to be thinking interesting thoughts. I don't mind doing boring tasks, but I simply don't know how to space out while I'm doing them. I can't switch my brain into idle while I'm stuck in line at the post office or while I'm

on hold, listening to elevator music. When I'm caught in traffic or mowing the lawn, I have to come up with some way to make the experience interesting to my mind.

I'm not just talking about simply distracting myself. We all naturally reach for the cell phone or bring up a solitaire game on the computer when we're forced to sit and wait. But when I try to distract myself this way, I get restless. The distraction bothers me just as much as the thing it's trying to distract me from. It's just how I'm wired. When my brain is on hold, I have this palpable sense of my life passing me by. It drives me crazy. So I am always trying to come up with ways to make things interesting.

For example:

Years ago when I first started doing long-distance runs, I would get terribly bored in the middle of them. I'd use up the supply of interesting thoughts that had been in my mind when I'd set out, and I'd become desperate for some sort of mental stimulation later. So, because I am also a musician, I started tuning in to the rhythm of the sounds that were most prominent to me: my footsteps and my breathing. I started by listening to the relatively even beat of my feet, in their march-like 4/4 meter. Then I tuned in to the much more irregular rhythms of my breathing, which might change from a waltzing 3/4 to an even more complex rhythm within a few paces. I tried to hear both rhythms simultaneously. I experimented with trying to

control the rhythms and then trying not to control them. I noticed how the rhythms evolved during the course of the run. I wondered whether there was some inherent pattern to these rhythms or whether they were simply random. I worked out musical compositions in my mind based on the evolving rhythms. I passed hours this way.

A lot of the exercises in this book have their origin in experiences like this. They are techniques that I have used in my own life to ground me and keep me focused and to make my life more interesting. Some of them I've developed over the years during work with my patients. Some have been derived directly from well-established psychotherapeutic interventions. But regardless of their origin, the process of their creation has been spontaneous, creative, and relatively unstructured.

In order to make these exercises as easily accessible as possible, I present them all in a standard format. Each is divided into five steps, followed by a brief meditation on themes suggested by the exercise. Following the instructions, I suggest a few variations on each exercise. Finally, I provide a list of books (or occasionally music) inspired by the exercise for further exploration.

The Power of Ten

It is important to me that these exercises can be done in the gaps and pauses of an ordinary day, so I have attempted

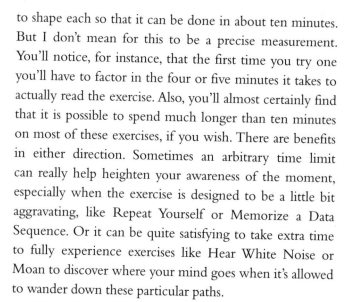

to shape each so that it can be done in about ten minutes. But I don't mean for this to be a precise measurement. You'll notice, for instance, that the first time you try one you'll have to factor in the four or five minutes it takes to actually read the exercise. Also, you'll almost certainly find that it is possible to spend much longer than ten minutes on most of these exercises, if you wish. There are benefits in either direction. Sometimes an arbitrary time limit can really help heighten your awareness of the moment, especially when the exercise is designed to be a little bit aggravating, like Repeat Yourself or Memorize a Data Sequence. Or it can be quite satisfying to take extra time to fully experience exercises like Hear White Noise or Moan to discover where your mind goes when it's allowed to wander down these particular paths.

The point is that these are simple exercises that can be done in a short space of time. But there's no need to limit yourself in any way. For instance, it can sometimes be very helpful to repeat an exercise in different situations. This is especially true if you find that a particular exercise resonates with you … for whatever reason. Try staying with it, repeating it as often as you like. Notice how the experience evolves with repetition. There are no hard and fast rules here. And there's also no risk. No harm can come from doing any of these exercises. You can trust your own intuition to guide you.

What Are These Based On, Anyway?

While they are unconventional in many ways, all these exercises are solidly based on psychological and philosophical principles. You'll find, for instance, many exercises that use strategies from cognitive-behavioral therapy (CBT), an approach that focuses on the ways in which our thoughts (especially automatic and self-critical thoughts) affect our emotions. According to this approach, by changing our thoughts, we can change how we feel.

You will also find many exercises that make use of the techniques of Gestalt therapy, an approach that emphasizes the importance of our direct, immediate experience over our cognitive interpretations of that experience. In Gestalt therapy, the therapist helps the patient focus on their experience in the here and now using techniques like exaggerating an inner sensation or physically enacting an inner experience.

I've certainly been influenced by motivational interviewing, a technique that harnesses the patients' own ambivalence as the foundation for change. And I've incorporated techniques from solution-focused therapy, which sees human change as inevitable and seeks to help patients identify the ways in which they are already making positive changes and then build on that foundation to construct the vision of the future that the patient desires.

I have, of course, drawn substantially from mindfulness-based approaches to therapy, such as those described in the writing of Jon Kabat-Zinn and Dan Siegel, that bring mindfulness meditation practice into the heart of the therapeutic work.

Finally, I am always powerfully influenced by my extensive postgraduate training in attachment theory and attachment-focused therapy. Attachment theory sheds tremendous light on the ways in which, through relationships, we develop the capacity for emotional regulation and for mindfulness itself. In the attachment literature, mindfulness is called "self-reflective functioning"—the ability of the mind to reflect on its own activity. I am convinced that it is this capacity (whether you want to call it mindfulness or self-reflective functioning or something else) that makes mental health, emotional maturity, and spiritual development possible. And strengthening this capacity is the goal of every one of the exercises in this book.

Mind Games

While there are no set rules for how and when you should use any of these exercises, the tasks themselves often suggest appropriate moments and places. Some, for instance, are based on physical or mental activities that you would be doing anyway and can be incorporated into the rhythms of your daily life. Some instruct you to

intentionally do things that you probably shouldn't do but inevitably will do anyway. Many have been designed so that you can do them entirely in your mind, easily and unobtrusively in the gaps that occur in an ordinary day. You can Dwell in the Past, for instance, while you're waiting for the bus. You can Look Around while you're riding in the elevator. A number of these exercises instruct you to engage in physical behavior that would seem bizarre if done in public. But I have found that those exercises work equally well when simply rehearsed mentally. This is in line with the growing body of research demonstrating that mentally rehearsing a performance (in music, for instance) activates the same brain regions that an actual rehearsal does, and provides an equivalent benefit to one's performance. Part of the beauty of these exercises is that mentally rehearsing them can provide the same shift in state of mind that a full enactment does.

How do you know which exercise to do at a particular moment? In many ways, it's not important. Each of these exercises will bring you, in its own way, to the same place: the here and now—the present moment. That's because beneath the very different nature of the many tasks in this book lies the same unifying principle: no matter what the activity, doing it with intention draws our awareness back to our center, to our own immediate experience. When we are observing our own minds in

action, we cannot help but be living in the present moment. And when we are living in the present, we cannot help but let go of everything we cannot control (e.g., the past and the present). As we center our attention on what we can control, we give ourselves full access to our own power, energy, and creativity.

While you might choose to read and do these exercises in the order they're presented, you're also free to browse through the table of contents and simply go to whatever catches your attention. You might open the book randomly to an exercise—Levitate, say—and then spend ten minutes trying to defy gravity. To further assist readers, I have included several appendices that loosely categorize the exercises into the sorts of feelings, problems, or goals that each addresses. If you're feeling constrained, for instance, I might suggest trying Pace. But keep in mind that these exercises often work in paradoxical ways. So if you're wanting to feel a sense of momentum, don't be surprised if I suggest that you Procrastinate or Dig in Your Heels, because sometimes the best way to get yourself to do something is to start by giving yourself permission not to do it.

Either way, whether you start on a random page or come to the book with a specific intention, the most constructive use of this book will be intuitive and spontaneous, playful and personal. Certainly these are the qualities I strive for as I work with my patients. I don't have a protocol

for how or when or in what order I use these exercises. Instead, I work creatively with whatever is happening in the therapeutic relationship in the present moment. Sometimes that means drawing on a specific exercise as it is outlined in this book, but just as often it means inventing a variation or an entirely new exercise on the spot.

Creative License

In using this book, I encourage you to trust your own impulses and to follow your intuition. That includes creating variations of these exercises that work for you and even making up your own. There are as many ways of going about this as there are individual experiences. We all have to wait in line, we all have to take out the trash, and we all just space out sometimes and stare at the wall. But no matter how similar these sorts of activities seem, your individual experience of them is always unique, and so will be the ways in which you activate your capacity for mindfulness in these moments.

While I'm confident that the act of reading this book and trying these exercises will naturally inspire you to invent your own variations on my technique, you might also like to take a more systematic approach to creating your own exercises. Why not start by simply observing yourself as you move through a typical day? Try keeping a log of all the gaps and pauses that you notice in your day.

(If you're feeling ambitious, you could also use a stopwatch to keep track of how much time you spend on each activity.) Make a separate list of the things that you have to do even though you'd rather be doing something else. And, of course, note the moments in your day when you feel fully alive and engaged.

At the end of the day, look through your log. Maybe you'll be appalled by what you discover or maybe you'll be energized. Either way I guarantee you that simply by observing yourself in this way you will begin to alter your state of mind. What patterns will you see? You might try presenting your data in a visual format. What would a pie graph of your day look like? A Venn diagram? How about a breakdown by frequency or length of activities?

Once you have gathered and organized your data, identify the parts of your day that seem most mundane, especially any parts that feel like "wasted time." Choose the activity or moment that bothers or intrigues you the most and write an instruction manual on how to perform this activity. Write it on as elementary a level as you can. Spell everything out in painstaking detail. As you do this, be sure to let your mind wander a little, because the way your mind wanders will instruct you about the ways in which you can make a mundane experience meaningful and interesting.

The important point here is that this book is meant as an inspiration to greater mindfulness, but it is only a

beginning. The practice of becoming more mindful within your everyday life naturally creates a positive feedback loop. Mindfulness leads to more mindfulness.

Finally, I invite you to share what you've created at www.thenexttenminutes.com. There you'll find a range of additional materials and conversations related to this book.

A Note to Professionals

This book evolved as an extension of techniques that I've used and found to be effective in work with my psychotherapy patients. If you're a therapist, it's my hope that you will find these ideas and techniques helpful as well, both for direct use in therapy and as homework for your patients. As should be apparent, I am more or less agnostic with regard to theoretical dogma. I don't believe that there is any single best approach to psychotherapy, and as I noted earlier, I have been quite eclectic in the development of these techniques, incorporating aspects of nearly every major approach to psychotherapy. Some might wonder if such eclecticism wouldn't simply create a chaotic and contradictory psychotherapeutic experience. But quite the opposite is true. The specific elements that I have drawn from different theories share a common goal that I believe is universal to all schools of psychotherapy: the enhancement of the individual's capacity to observe his or her own mind in action.

So no matter what your theoretical orientation, I feel confident that you will find ideas and techniques here that you already use in some form in your own practice. More importantly, I believe you will find ideas within these techniques that allow you to see your usual interventions in deeper and more creative ways. As therapists, we are prone to settle into routines just as much as our patients do. And so the strategies underlying these exercises can also be applied to the practice of therapy itself. We always can become more mindful of our own therapeutic practice. It's my hope that the techniques in this book will allow and encourage you to sharpen and deepen the strategies that you are already using, improving patient outcomes, enlivening your practice, and providing you with more satisfaction in your work.

This has been the result in my own practice. As I use these techniques with my patients, I notice distinct benefits in several ways. First, the exercises are disorienting. This in and of itself is often beneficial, especially for patients suffering from depressive disorders. We typically expend a great deal of energy trying to help such patients (depending on our particular theoretical orientation) externalize their depression or identify the critical voice that is locking the depression in place. These exercises are designed to slip in the back door, so to speak, to get the patient into a different state of mind before he or she even

realizes that it's happening. Once the patient has demonstrated the capacity to control his or her own state of mind, the door is wide open to a deeper exploration of the sources of the depression and the strategies for fighting it.

Second (and not unrelated to the previous point), these exercises are inherently optimistic. Even (or perhaps especially) when they are paradoxically encouraging patients to magnify their own symptoms, they all share the same underlying philosophy: that people already have within themselves what they need in order to make positive changes in their lives. Every exercise insists that the patient is the author of his or her own narrative and that he or she is ultimately in charge of the direction that story will take. I find that this aspect of the exercises is particularly important with regard to those suffering from anxiety disorders. In such patients, I have seen again and again how this empowering narrative improves their ability to more realistically assess the triggers of their anxiety, increases their capacity for regulating strong emotions, and generally stimulates a greater sense of self-confidence.

Finally, these exercises all facilitate (sometimes rather indirectly) an enhanced capacity for emotional regulation. This is yet another benefit of the mindfulness practices that underlie the exercises, encouraging patients to train their minds to observe their thoughts and emotions with-

out reacting to them. While emotional regulation is a necessity for mental health in general, I have found this aspect of the exercises to be particularly important to work involving relationship issues. As one example, much of my own clinical work is with individual men in conjunction with concurrent marital therapy provided by another therapist. Many men suffer from what researchers have labeled "normative alexithymia"—the inability to name their emotions. And this difficulty is commonly a source of great distress and conflict within a marriage. These exercises address this issue by engaging men in a sort of "laboratory" experiment of their own experiences. Creating this experimental distance allows men a safe way to explore and identify their emotional experiences and opens the door to more constructive ways to understand and communicate those emotions.

These are just a few of the many ways in which these exercises can benefit your patients and enliven your practice. While the results of these sorts of techniques may not be readily captured by outcome studies, they are, as I described earlier, the butterfly's wing that ultimately can cause a distant storm. I believe that their observed effectiveness is in line with the growing body of research on the benefit of mindfulness training in psychotherapy.

I use these techniques in a spontaneous and creative manner; I have not developed them as part of a formal

therapeutic protocol (nor do I believe that they could be used in such a way). But that's not to say that they are meant to be used casually or without an explicit goal. They're fun to use, but the goal is to foster and enhance a patient's capacity for self-reflective functioning. With this in mind, I have designed these exercises so that they can be incorporated into work with patients experiencing a broad range of issues. And while judgment is always required in the choice and timing of therapeutic interventions, I don't believe that there are any disorders for which these exercises are unconditionally contraindicated. In fact, I have developed some of these exercises conjointly with trauma survivors in the midst of some very intense de-conditioning work (Animate a Memory is the clearest example).

In writing this book, it's been my desire to share what I've learned with as wide an audience as possible and to stimulate further conversation about ways in which we can help foster positive change in our patients. It's my hope that these exercises will not only help your patients make a shift into a state of greater mindfulness, but also that it will spark further creativity and discussion among professionals. I invite you to share these exercises with your own patients and to share your own ideas and join with me in the conversation at www.thenexttenminutes.com.

1

Procrastinate

Make use of the secret technique that all therapists learn on their first day of training: in situations where there is no imminent danger (i.e., nearly all the time), doing nothing will cause no harm.

What You'll Need
- A pressing task from your daily life

How to Do It
1. **Choose a task.** Identify what feels like the most stressful thing that you should be doing right at this moment. It doesn't have to be an objectively important task. Ideally it will be something you feel *external* pressure to do. But what matters most is that it is creating stress in your life. It might be an apology you know you need to make or bills that need paying.
2. **Focus on the task.** Don't try to ignore it or put it out of your mind. (That is an advanced step that can come

once you've mastered the basic technique.) Feel all the pressure that comes with the task and all the emotions that come from not doing it. Imagine your loved ones all around you, looking on with disappointment, clucking their tongues and lovingly scolding you.

3. Vigorously fail to do the task. *Refuse* to do it.

4. Pause. Take a deep, slow breath. Notice whatever thoughts and feelings rush in. Notice what happens in your body. Say to yourself, "I will do it in ten minutes." Repeat this phrase as often as necessary, continuing to focus on the task that you aren't doing.

5. Go about your business. It is irrelevant to the success of this exercise whether you return to the task or whether you ever actually get it done.

Embracing the Stress

There are plenty of people out there who will tell you that the art of procrastination is an antidote to the stresses and pressures of modern life. In general, the idea is that you should give yourself permission to delay doing things *without guilt* and let yourself indulge fully in a sense of lazy relaxation. This approach to procrastination misses the point. It's like telling someone who's depressed that they should just try to be happier. If you are able to *truly* avoid thinking about things you're supposed to be doing, then it's not actually procrastination.

In order to experience the true benefits of procrastination, you've got to really embrace the stress. Because procrastination isn't about "doing nothing"; it's about *not* doing "something." Ten minutes of procrastination is good for you not because it's relaxing, but because you're acknowledging the reality of your life and acknowledging your power to act ... or not.

Variations: Other Ways to *Not* Do Things

Experiment with distractions. The natural impulse when going about our daily, usually unconscious practice of procrastinating is to try to avoid awareness of the thing we're supposed to be doing. The basic version of this exercise intentionally eliminates distraction in order to heighten the experience of procrastinating. Once you have mastered the basic exercise, however, it can be very enlightening to reintroduce distraction. Do the first two steps of the exercise as described; then at step three, try to force yourself to think about a subject that has nothing to do with the task at hand. Start with easy distractions, such as food, sex, and money. Then move on to more boring—and thus more challenging—distractions. Are you able to distract yourself from an important task by focusing on balancing your checkbook?

Use visual aids. (For advanced practitioners only.) These are the big guns of procrastination, and when we're

trying to put something off, we usually go for them first. Computer games, the internet—using these things to procrastinate is like taking heroin to cure a headache. They work so effectively that they don't give us the opportunity to experience the full spectrum of the procrastination experience. Using these sorts of tools to procrastinate will call on all your skills, so make sure to master the basic techniques first.

Do it, but only halfheartedly. A final way to vary this exercise involves harnessing your capacity for passive-aggressive behavior. Don't procrastinate, but don't do the task well either. We all do this at times, but usually we do it more or less unconsciously. Try bringing full awareness to a task while you're doing a half-assed job on it. Can you stay focused on your refusal to do the task well even as you are doing it?

Further Reading: In Praise of Inaction

- Tom Hodgkinson, *How to Be Idle*, Harper Perennial, 2007.
- Tom Lutz, *Doing Nothing: A History of Loafers, Loungers, Slackers, and Bums in America*, Farrar, Straus and Giroux, 2007.
- Bertrand Russell, *In Praise of Idleness and Other Essays*, Routledge, 2004.

2

Relax Your Face

Sounds easy, right? But try relaxing your face for more than a few seconds and you'll quickly realize how hard your face is working at every moment. Even when you're completely alone, your face is busily exercising its muscles, subtly (or not so subtly) expressing your inner state. Because our facial muscles are regulated by our social experiences, they're deeply enmeshed with our thought processes. As a result, maintaining relaxed facial muscles requires a shift in our state of mind. Here's how to start making that shift.

What You'll Need
•   Your face

How to Do It
1. **Observe your face in its natural state.** Stop right there! Before you change anything about your face, take a moment to catch your facial muscles unaware.

What are they doing right now? Don't look in the mirror; just feel them and notice. What are your jaw muscles up to? How about the muscles around your eyes? Your forehead?

2. **Scrunch it up.** Though it seems paradoxical, the best way to relax any muscle is to start by tensing it. This is because it's so difficult to make ourselves aware of the tension that we're holding in our muscles until we feel the contrast between tension and relaxation. Try to tighten all the different muscles in your face at once. As you do this, your neck muscles will start to shake, making your entire head vibrate. You'll look pretty strange, but that's all right. No one is watching.

3. **Relax.** Resist the urge to release the tension all at once. Let it go *slowly*. Remember that you're trying to feel the contrast between the tense and the relaxed muscle, so the point here is to observe the transformation as it occurs. The first phase of relaxation will feel easy and pleasurable. But don't stop there. Keep the momentum, using slow breathing, urging yourself into deeper facial relaxation. You'll probably notice muscles in the rest of your body starting to relax as well. That's great, but don't focus on it. Keep your attention on your face. Close your eyes and imagine your muscles melting as you feel your face go utterly slack.

4. **Hold it right there.** Keep your eyes closed and maintain this relaxed state. Picture the face of a sleeping infant, completely empty of care. You should be feeling pretty good right about now. Your face works so hard all the time. You're giving it a little vacation.

5. **Keep holding it.** Now, here comes the interesting part. After a minute or two, your mind is going to get restless. It's going to want to *do* something, so it's going to start harassing you with thoughts. With these thoughts is going to come a retightening of your various facial muscles. Try to hold on to your relaxed state, but notice the subtle shifts that thoughts create in your facial musculature. A passing cynical thought ("This is stupid.") might raise your cheek and lip muscles on one side. A fleeting sexual fantasy might tighten your lips into a slight smile. Try to catch these shifts as they happen, and relax your face again. It's probably going to feel like a game of Whac-A-Mole, but keep going until you can't stand it anymore. Then release your face back to its normal duties and go about your day.

The Subterranean Choreography of Our Musculature

It can be remarkably difficult to make yourself accurately aware of the state of your own musculature. I can still

remember an introductory gymnastics class that I took as a child in which the instructor had each of us drape ourselves over a bar on our stomach. Then he told us to fully relax our legs. I watched each child ahead of me as the teacher asked, "Are your legs fully relaxed?" Yes, they answered, but it was obvious that they weren't; they were thrust out stiffly in an unconscious effort to maintain a sense of balance. When my turn came, I was certain that I had figured out the trick. But it made no difference. I responded in exactly the same way as the other kids had. I could not override my body's impulse to remain rigid. How much of our experience is unconsciously shaped by this subterranean muscular choreography? How possible is it to become conscious of our own muscles?

Variations: Reading Faces

Practice progressive muscle relaxation. This exercise is a variation on one of the simplest and most effective relaxation techniques I know—one you can learn to use in just a few minutes. Simply isolate different muscle groups (it can be a large group, like your entire left leg, or you can break it into smaller sets, starting, say, with the toes on your left foot); then tighten those muscles and hold the squeeze for ten to twenty seconds. Breathe steadily as you gently release the tension, feeling the contrasting relaxation. Take another slow breath before moving on to the next muscle group. Gradually move across your entire body; then notice the change in your physical and mental state when you are done.

Consider your thoughts. Cognitive psychologists like to talk about how thoughts create emotions, because this means that changing how we think can change how we feel. But as this exercise demonstrates, thoughts also create specific physical states—in our faces and in the rest of our bodies. Experiment with this by trying out different thoughts and noticing the physical reaction each creates. What happens when you think angry thoughts? How about a positive affirmation? Try jealousy, grief, delight, and confusion, and see what happens.

Become a face reader. The research of Paul Ekman has made it possible for us to break the code of facial expressions. We all are intuitively reading people's facial expressions all the time, but are we doing so accurately? How can we tell, for instance, when someone is lying? Ekman has broken down emotions into their muscular components and made it possible for us to become scientific in the way we look at other people's faces. It's hard to do, but it's fascinating to try.

Further Reading: About Face
* Brian Bates with John Cleese, *The Human Face*, Dorling Kindersley, 2001.

- Paul Ekman and Wallace V. Friesen, *Unmasking the Face: A Guide to Recognizing Emotions from Facial Clues*, Malor Books, 2003.
- Lucy Grealy, *Autobiography of a Face*, Harper Perennial, 2003.
- Mark Simon, *Facial Expressions: A Visual Reference for Artists*, Watson-Guptill, 2005.

3

Go into Another Room

This exercise is a variation on the old joke about the guy who goes to the doctor and says, "It hurts when I do this." You know already what you need to do to create change in your life, but sometimes you just need a doctor telling you to do it.

What You'll Need
• A building with more than one room

How to Do It
1. **Pick a room.** It doesn't matter which, although preferably it will be one that you have already been in for at least a few minutes.
2. **Stay where you are.** This is very important. It will be tempting to jump straight to step 4, but for the exercise to be effective, you must begin by remaining in your current position. Take a breath. Notice the sensations in your body. Then notice the feel of the air in the

room. Is it cool or warm? Dry or damp? Is the air circulating or still? Next, move your focus out through the space of the room to the walls. Do they feel embracing or confining? Constricting or spacious? Take it all in.

3. **Listen.** Close your eyes while you do this. Even if there are no sounds in the room, your ears can detect a great deal about the qualities of the room. What are the acoustics? Muffled? Boomy? Can you "hear" how far away the walls are? Clap your hands together and listen to the reverberations.

4. **Go into a different room.** Open your eyes. If you are sitting, stand up. Take a breath and walk slowly into a different room. As you walk, notice the feel of the space as it changes around you. Pay special attention to sensations you experience as you pass through the doorway. The transition between rooms takes place in just a brief moment. See if you can slow down your awareness enough to detect the sensation of the transition as it happens.

5. **Explore the new room.** When you arrive in the new room, sit or stand as you please. Take a slow breath, exhale, and then repeat steps 2–3 in reverse order. Close your eyes and experience the acoustics of the room. Open your eyes and notice the space of the room, starting with the walls and working inward toward the

center. Finally, attune to the sensation in your own body as you experience this new room.

Do Something Different

As a psychotherapist, sometimes this is the most useful thing I can tell someone. It sounds too simple to be effective, but often it actually helps. And paradoxically, sometimes it helps the most when we don't focus on the problem itself. That's because when we focus on changing a behavior that is emotionally charged (looking at internet pornography, say, or overeating), we are already so invested in the future outcome that we skip over the crucial truth about any personal change. But in order to change your future behavior, you've first got to change your *present* state of mind. That's why intentionally forcing yourself to change a random and insignificant behavior can be so valuable. Once you shift your awareness away from the future and attend to your own behavior in the present moment, many new things become possible.

Variations: Other Ways to Move

Do it in the dark. Enhance your awareness of the non-visual aspects of different rooms by doing this exercise at night with the lights out.

Go outside. Outdoor spaces also have their own particular qualities. The basic version of this exercise asks you to become aware of what can be very subtle shifts in tone between different spaces. Once you have trained yourself to be more sensitive to these differences, you can heighten the effect by doing the exercise while moving to or from the outdoors.

Stay in the room, but change it. It's entirely possible that in the course of doing this exercise you'll discover that there's something about particular rooms in your life that just don't feel right. Maybe it's the arrangement of the furniture. Maybe it needs de-cluttering. Maybe a window needs opening. You can use this exercise as a springboard to improving the spaces you inhabit.

Further Reading: How Architectural Spaces Influence Our Experiences

- Barry Blesser and Linda-Ruth Salter, *Spaces Speak, Are You Listening?: Experiencing Aural Architecture*, MIT Press, 2007.
- Alain de Botton, *The Architecture of Happiness*, Pantheon, 2006.

4

Move as if You Are Underwater

Moving in slow motion interrupts the numbed, thought-less activity of our bodies, making it intentional, purposeful, and experienced. It's profoundly simple but, as you'll discover in this exercise, surprisingly difficult to sustain for more than a few minutes.

What You'll Need
- An everyday task
- Patience

How to Do It
1. **Choose a task.** Make it something simple and undemanding, like peeling carrots, dusting the furniture, or folding laundry.
2. **Create the illusion.** Take a long, slow breath. Close your eyes and imagine that you are underwater. Feel the pressure against your skin. Let the water be warm and gentle, exquisitely comfortable.

3. **Go to work.** Open your eyes and consider the task. Take your time. When you're ready, consciously direct your body to begin moving. Make each movement deliberate. Tell your left arm to move slowly toward the carrot. Tell your left hand to open and grab the carrot, to hold it in the air. Tell your right arm to move toward the peeler. And so on. You'll discover that physical movements are infinitely divisible. Don't agonize over this; just see how microscopically you can consciously divide your physical movements. Remember that it's not so much about moving *slowly* as it is about moving *deliberately*.

4. **Continue.** You will find that as your mind wanders, you'll start speeding up unintentionally. That's fine; don't worry. Just bring your thoughts gently back to the slow-motion task.

5. **Move on.** When ten minutes are up, ease your way back toward a normal pace, but feel free to continue moving at a slightly slower speed if that feels right. You may continue the task you started or move on to something new.

What to Do with Your Brain

In this exercise you are called on to transform automatic physical movements into conscious, intentional behavior. Ordinarily, our bodies take care of this for us, leaving our minds free to do other things. Everything's reversed here, as our mind is tethered back to our physical body. Your brain is going to resist this like crazy. This is not actually a problem. For this exercise to be beneficial, all you need to do is to make the effort. But one way to help your mind is to use a repeated sound or phrase. Buddhists like to say that the mind is like a yapping dog, and that using a repeated sound or phrase—a mantra—is like tossing a bone to the dog to help it quiet down. In this case, you might say something like, "Slowly, slowly, slowly."

Variations: Life in Slow Motion

Increase complexity. The point of picking everyday tasks to start with is to give your brain the best opportunity to let go of its insistent need for dominance as you briefly bind it to the movement of your body. As you become more skilled, try increasing the complexity of the tasks. This will call on your mind to engage simultaneously in its usual complex cognitive processing and in the much more mechanical monitoring of your physical movements.

Do it in public. This is a high-level skill, one that is best exemplified by hypermilers—people who practice driving techniques meant to squeeze the most mileage possible out of their vehicles. Hypermiling is essentially driving underwater. It is exquisitely challenging to combine the

complexity of real-time driving with intentionally slow physical behavior. Driving is such a complex activity, in fact, that you'll probably want to consider starting with a simpler physical activity. Try taking a slow-motion walk in the park. Go shopping in slow motion. If you get interrupted, don't worry about it. Just shift back into your regular speed.

Join the slow food movement. It's a revolutionary idea: start tasting your food again. The impulse to eat quickly undoubtedly dates back to our troglodyte days, when food was hard to come by and the ability to consume it quickly gave us an evolutionary advantage. But we're not troglodytes anymore. Try combining the pleasure of eating with the intensity of moving in slow motion and find out what you've been missing.

Further Reading: Slow Is the New Fast

- Cecile Andrews, *Slow Is Beautiful: New Visions of Community, Leisure and Joie de Vivre*, New Society Publishers, 2006.

- Carl Honoré, *In Praise of Slowness: How a Worldwide Movement Is Challenging the Cult of Speed*, HarperOne, 2004.

- Carlo Petrini, *Slow Food Nation: Why Our Food Should Be Good, Clean, and Fair*, Rizzoli Ex Libris, 2007.

5

Memorize a Data Sequence

On March 14, Pi Day, my son's middle school class had a contest to see who could memorize the most digits of pi. One of his classmates was able to memorize the figure to sixty-five decimal places. That's 3.14159265358979323846 26433832795028841971693993751058209749444592 30. As a result of her skill, she got to be the first to choose a slice of the many pies that parents had brought in for the occasion. The delightfully pointless nature of the contest, combined with the sweet reward, awakened me to the pleasures of random short-term memorization. While "rote memorization" has been much derided as an educational technique, it's undeniable that the mechanics of memory form the foundation of our capacity for higher-order thinking. Please, though, don't mistake this exercise for a memory-enhancement program. The goal here is not to increase your memory or to improve your performance on standardized tests. The goal of this exercise is to experience the encoding mechanisms of your brain in their most elemental forms. And maybe even to win a piece of pie.

What You'll Need

- Your full attention (or something close to it)
- A piece of information, written on a piece of paper

How to Do It

1. **Pick a piece of information.** It can be verbal or numerical, but preferably it will be something without any inherent meaning in your life. Try using a list of ingredients on a package of heavily processed food, the instructions for self-assembly furniture (preferably translated from a foreign language), or the chronological order of ancient Chinese dynasties.

2. **Study the first element in the sequence.** Let's say it's "calcium carbonate." Try to hear it the way you would if it were in a foreign language. Say it out loud, slowly, letting your mind turn the syllables into a meaningless string of sound.

3. **Study the second element.** When the first element has been transformed in your mind, move on to the second. Say it's "pomegranate juice." Repeat step 2 with this phrase. Try to focus on it entirely, without making any effort to remember the first element.

4. **Combine the elements.** Once you have reduced this second phrase to a series of tones in your mind, try to mentally retrieve the first element. Since you haven't tried to memorize it, what you're looking for is the echo of it in the back of your mind. When you have found it (feel free to look it up if necessary), say the two elements together, listening to the tonal combinations: cal-ci-um-car-bon-ate-pome-gran-ate-juice.

5. **Repeat.** Don't worry about how far you get. Memorizing two or three elements will work just as well as memorizing nine or ten. After you're done, don't try to hang on to the information. Let it all wash away.

Meaning and Meaninglessness

There are lots of great techniques for teaching yourself to memorize information. Don't use any of them for this exercise. Instead, rely on cognitive brute force. Try to force your mind to hold the sequence of information without making any associative connections. This can be very hard to do, as it is in the nature of our minds to create meaning even when none is inherently present. In fact, this makes the very task of identifying a "meaningless" data sequence quite challenging. But the point here is to try to resist the natural power of our minds to create meaning. In this way, we can begin to push our minds

into new territory, which connects us to the primal and revitalizing sensation of non-meaning.

Variations: Memory on the Run

Extend the task over time. In the basic version of this exercise, you are intentionally not trying to retain this information in your long-term memory. But it is always interesting to discover how much gets stored there even when you're not trying, which is why coming back to the same piece of meaningless information over time can yield interesting results. Can you experience the information as something new, even though you've previously memorized it?

Do it on the move. I knew a guy in college who had memorized how many steps there were in every staircase on campus. You can use memorization as a sort of Zen "walking meditation." Memorize the sequence of street names as you drive down the street or the order of the stores in the mall. This increases the challenge because it's much more difficult to check whether or not you're remembering things accurately. Once it leaves your memory, it's gone.

Forget about it. Amnesia is the flip side of memorization, and it can be an equally difficult state to attain. Try moving through the world for a few minutes as if you could remember nothing about your life and as if you had

no capacity to remember anything that was happening to you in the present.

Further Reading: Exploring the Mysteries of Memory

- Eric R. Kandel, *In Search of Memory: The Emergence of a New Science of Mind*, W. W. Norton, 2006.
- Jill Price with Bart Davis, *The Woman Who Can't Forget: The Extraordinary Story of Living with the Most Remarkable Memory Known to Science—A Memoir*, Free Press, 2008.
- Daniel L. Schacter, *The Seven Sins of Memory: How the Mind Forgets and Remembers*, Mariner Books, 2002.

Throw Something Away

Although it feels like heresy to say it in these days of maniacal recycling and composting, sometimes trash is really just trash. It's a truth of the world that our existence creates waste products. Rather than getting mired in anxiety about the waste you create, take a moment to awaken to the deeper rhythms of the life cycle embedded in your daily existence by bringing your full awareness to a single piece of genuine garbage as you dispose of it.

What You'll Need
- Something that needs to be thrown away

How to Do It
1. **Select the object.** It needs to be true trash—something that really *has* to go to the landfill. It can't be something that you could donate to a good cause or sell on eBay. If you recycle (and you *should*, of course), it can't be something that could be recycled in any way.

Food scraps or vegetable matter are okay, unless you have a compost pile. Take your time picking an object; figuring out how to define "true trash" is part of the exercise. Feel free to look into the garbage can for inspiration, but no fair taking something out that you've already thrown away!

2. **Contemplate the object's history.** Whether it's organic or human-made, every object has a story. Maybe it's the story of the seed that grows into the tree that gets cut down and made into wooden chopsticks. Maybe it's the story of the oil that is turned into plastic and shaped into a comb. Maybe you can't possibly comprehend how the object came into existence; if so, feel free to make something up.

3. **Contemplate the object's future.** Will it decompose? If so, how and where? And what will come of the components of the goo that it turns into? If it's not likely to break down any time soon, extend the time frame. What will archaeologists make of it hundreds or thousands of years from now?

4. **Give the object a funeral.** Honor its passing. Express your appreciation for the role the object has played in your life and in the world. Then acknowledge that all things die.

5. **Throw it away.** Feel how simple the actual gesture is, in contrast to the deep thinking that you have been

doing as part of this exercise. Let yourself experience the release and freedom that is inextricably linked to loss and transformation.

You and Your Waste

Children are much better at this than grown-ups. They can talk about waste products with gusto. But for them, garbage is a potential toy. And, of course, they have great books like *Everyone Poops* to help them along. Most of us adults avoid becoming fully aware of our relationship to our own waste, whether it's material, biological, or emotional. In fact, I suspect that more than a few of us have nearly completely banished the awareness that we produce any waste at all. That's why the really interesting question here isn't so much what happens to *garbage* after we throw it away, but rather what happens to *us* in the act of throwing something away. And that's also why, no matter how silly it seems, each act of disposal is also an opportunity for awakening to a deeper truth about our deeper nature: human existence is a continuous process of letting go.

Variations: Dig Deeper

Keep a garbage log. Experience the full extent of your involvement with trash by taking a few days to keep track of all the waste you generate. Do it without judgment and simply as an exercise in awareness.

Imagine deep reuse. What if there were some way to make use of everything that you now toss into the garbage can? Use your imagination (and let yourself go to absurd lengths) to create a new use for everything you throw away.

Become an amateur garbologist. Perhaps you remember the advent of popular garbology, when news reporters started going through famous people's trash to uncover secrets from their personal lives. This made a lot of people uncomfortable, because garbage straddles the fuzzy line between public and private. But you don't need to go dumpster diving to develop a deeper understanding of the secret life of trash (although if you're interested, there are entire books written about the practice). All you really need to do is take a walk through the alleys around your house and notice what's on top of your neighbors' garbage cans.

Practice anticipatory decomposition. Imagining the future of your trash, especially when you include garbologists in the mix, can create anxiety. What would people think about me if they went through my trash? Start erasing the evidence by shredding your important documents before you throw them out. But don't stop there; try to imagine the natural process of decomposition and think about what you can do to hasten it.

Further Reading: Books on Garbage and Waste

- Rose George, *The Big Necessity: The Unmentionable World of Human Waste and Why It Matters*, Metropolitan Books, 2008.
- Taro Gomi, *Everyone Poops*, Kane/Miller Book Publishers, 2001.
- John Hoffman, *The Art and Science of Dumpster Diving*, Palladin Press, 1993.
- William Rathje and Cullen Murphy, *Rubbish!: The Archaeology of Garbage*, University of Arizona Press, 2001.

7

Take Baby Steps

Imagine how much you used to not know. There was a time in your existence when someone leaving the room meant that they literally disappeared. There was a time when you heard the sounds of speech without being able to decipher them. Bring back that primitive experience of not knowing by re-creating the experience of learning how to walk.

What You'll Need
- An open space with a soft floor
- Something to pull yourself up on

How to Do It
1. **Forget what you know.** This is the hardest part of the exercise. It's like trying to forget how to ride a bike. It's not really possible, but do your best to approximate for-gettting by lying down on the floor on your stomach and concentrating all your energy into your abdominal

muscles. Let your legs simply flail and let little spasms of energy rush through them in the form of short kicks, but don't try to control your leg muscles any more than this. While you're down on the floor, make sure to take in the view from this perspective; this is what the world used to look like to you.

2. **Push up.** Use your arms to raise your shoulders as far as you can. Then, slowly, remembering that you don't have much physical control, pull your legs up underneath you and into a crawling position. Try crawling across the room. Let yourself be hesitant at first, moving one limb at a time. Take a minute or two to reenact the experience of learning to crawl quickly. Crawling babies can move incredibly fast. Can you do the same thing now?

3. **Pull yourself to a standing position.** Feeling the increased coordination that you developed in the last step, use your arms to pull yourself up to a stand. Let your legs be shaky, though; they're not used to feeling the full weight of your body. See if you can undo the deeply ingrained sense of balance so that as you let go with your arms, you feel unsteady, uncertain whether you'll be able to remain upright.

4. **Take a step.** Imagination is the key here. Don't worry about what you may or may not know about your actual first step. Here I want you to try to imagine the

most stereotypical scene: Put yourself in a Norman Rockwell painting. Two perfect parents—not *your* parents—wait a few feet away from you, with arms open. Move one leg deliberately forward. Feel the space between you and the adults as a vast ocean. Wobble a bit.

5. **Fall.** This is perhaps the most important part of the exercise. Don't let yourself resume your normal walking ability without first experiencing how fragile and hard-won it originally was. Imagine what it means to fall as an infant. Let yourself collapse on the floor. Then imagine those ideal adults sweeping down on you, filled with love and pride.

Pathways

We have come to think of walking as something utterly simple. It's such a deeply internalized physical action that it is nearly impossible to recover the complex mechanics of walking from our unconscious. For the most part, that's a good thing. If you had to remain as conscious of the mechanics of walking as you do during this exercise, you'd have a hard time moving forward through your life.

What's really interesting here is how hard it is to move backward through our own development. We know that we didn't used to know how to do this thing, but we no longer have access to what that experience

was like. The neural pathways that guide our motor activities have been so strongly imprinted in our minds that it's nearly impossible to willfully unlearn the behavior, which is why the most important variable in this exercise is your imagination.

Variations: Next Steps

Variations for those with physical impairments. Because imagination is the key to this exercise, there's no reason you can't do it even if you are physically unable to walk. Try doing it entirely in your imagination. This can be just as powerful as enacting it physically. Another variation involves using different motor activities—throwing a ball, drawing simple shapes, and so on. You can apply the principle of this exercise to any learned physical action.

Walking meditation. This classic Buddhist meditation technique merges mindfulness meditation with the simple physical activity of walking. Check out Thich Nhat Hanh for guidance (see the books listed at the end of this exercise).

Run. The physical complications of walking mindfully are multiplied when you apply the techniques in this exercise to the act of running. Start with a simple lope, trying to be aware of the muscular mechanics that make running possible. Be aware of your body, but also remain alert to your surroundings.

Further Reading: Books on Walking

- Joseph A. Amato, *On Foot: A History of Walking*, New York University Press, 2004.
- Colin Fletcher and Chip Rawlins, *The Complete Walker IV*, Knopf, 2002.
- Thich Nhat Hanh, *The Long Road Turns to Joy: A Guide to Walking Meditation*, Parallax Press, 1996.
- Geoff Nicholson, *The Lost Art of Walking: The History, Science, and Literature of Pedestrianism*, Riverhead Books, 2008.

8

Animate a Memory

I once worked with a patient who had suffered terrible trauma during a car accident. Every time he heard the sound of wheels screeching, even if it was blocks away, he would go into a full-blown panic attack. I struggled to help him find a way to override his brain's innate tendency to give priority to signals of perceived danger. But he came up with an ingenious way of handling these flashbacks. He decided that whenever he heard that sound, he would turn the scene into a cartoon in his mind. He would picture Road Runner pulling up to a screeching stop in front of Wile E. Coyote. *Beep beep!* The image, when set against his actual memory, was so absurd that it made him laugh ... and it interrupted the flashback. You can use this same technique for everyday memories and events; the effects are delightfully unpredictable and invigorating.

What You'll Need
- An ordinary memory

How to Do It

1. **Choose a memory.** To start with, pick a small irritating moment from your life, a *specific* instance of something that happens on a regular basis. (You want to be sure to have the opportunity to use the technique in the future.) It might be something like your spouse's snoring, being cut off in traffic, or a co-worker's nosy questions. It doesn't matter too much what it is, but do keep it simple, even mundane. Try to resist the temptation to pick something upsetting or traumatic from your past. (While you're learning this technique, it's best to use a memory with minimal emotional charge so that it's easier to manipulate. Later you can apply the technique to more challenging memories.)

2. **Shape the memory into a story.** Even though the memory you've chosen is simple, it can still be shaped into a small story. (Remember how clearly defined each vignette is in a Road Runner episode.) Start by setting the scene. Give some background on the characters involved. Every good story has a central conflict, so define that clearly. Then let the conflict play out into some sort of resolution.

3. **Choose your cartoon characters.** I recommend using classic cartoon characters to enact the memory, but whatever works for you is fine. You might pick characters that seem appropriate to the story (like

Dudley Do-Right for a traffic cop who gave you a speeding ticket). Or you might simply pick characters who make you smile when you think of them.

4. **Transform the memory.** Here's the fun part: Recast the narrative you just created with the cartoon characters chosen in step 3. Now use your imagination, replay the story in your mind, and let loose. Let the goofy energy of the cartoon characters infuse the story. Say you've cast Daffy Duck as a nosy co-worker and Bugs Bunny as you. Let yourself unleash a barrage of insane behavior. Take it to extremes. Resolve the conflict in the most hilarious way you can possibly imagine.

5. **Create a switch.** Before you end, take a moment to set up a mental "switch" that you can use the next time this event happens in real life. Picture the real-life scene taking place. Then identify a small physical gesture that you can use to "turn on" the cartoon. It should be something you can do more or less imperceptibly, like the motion of turning on a light switch or pressing a button on a remote control. The next time the event happens, see if you can "flip the switch" and transform it into the cartoon version in your mind.

Changing Your Mind

This exercise is all about the power of your mind to shape your experiences. When you shift your state of mind—for

better or for worse—you change your judgment of the things around you. The guy who cuts you off in traffic on the way home from work appears different on the day you just got a raise than on the day you just got laid off. *He's* the same but your assessment of him is different. And that's where we get into trouble: we mistake our assessment of the world for reality itself.

Changing your perception really can happen in the space of a few minutes. But while the process of change is simple, it's not always easy to achieve. Our minds are strangely wedded to our habitual ways of perceiving the world, even when this is making us unhappy. This exercise is a sort of shortcut that will, over time, give you more and more power to control your own state of mind.

Variations: Expand Your Technique

Draw it. There is something fundamentally satisfying about a comic strip. The entire world is reduced to elemental sketches in a three- or four-frame story. In that format, everything starts to seem manageable. Don't worry if you can't draw well; in fact, that can actually be an advantage here. I, for one, have absolutely no talent for drawing, but when my children were young, I had them make up stories that I would then illustrate as cartoons. My illustrations were absurdly awful, but this actually made them a perfect match for the crazy stories my kids would tell.

Real-time animation. The basic version of this exercise relies on the power of reflection. Looking back on a specific event while shaping it into a narrative gives you control over the meaning that you assign to it. The ultimate goal you're after, however, is to be able to control your own state of mind in the present moment. You can do this by experimenting with using this exercise in real time, imagining scenes and events as cartoons as they are happening. This requires you to hold two versions of reality in your mind at once, so it can be extra challenging at times.

More difficult memories. I learned this technique as a way to cope with powerful traumatic memories, and it works very well for this purpose. Once you've mastered the basic technique, try applying it to more challenging memories. Don't immediately jump to the worst thing you've ever experienced, though. Do it incrementally. When I'm working with trauma victims, I start by looking at the big picture. I ask them to describe *all* the things associated with the specific traumatic event. Then we start working with the easiest one. I encourage you to take the same approach. Make a short list of the difficult memories and then rank them in order of how upsetting they are to you. Start with the easiest one and learn to get control of it before you move to the next memory. You'll know you've mastered each memory

when you can think about it with full awareness of the emotions it arouses but without having those emotions infect your current state of mind.

Further Reading: Explore the Science Behind Changing Your Mind

- Sharon Begley, *Train Your Mind, Change Your Brain: How a New Science Reveals Our Extraordinary Potential to Transform Ourselves*, Ballantine Books, 2007.
- Norman Doidge, MD, *The Brain That Changes Itself: Stories of Personal Triumph from the Frontiers of Brain Science*, Penguin, 2007.

9

Stare at the Wall

I don't understand why staring at the wall has gotten such a bad reputation. It's your existential right to practice this fundamental experience of doing nothing. Stare at the wall with purpose, and let the blankness in front of you reveal the lush and lively activity within your own mind.

What You'll Need
• A blank painted wall

How to Do It
1. **Situate yourself.** The wall that you select should have nothing hanging on it. It should be painted, not wallpapered. A single, solid color is best. The wall also needs to be accessible and large enough so that you can stand about six to eight inches away from it—close enough that there's nothing else in your field of vision. Minimize distractions: turn off the music and silence your cell phone. You're going to put yourself in a bit

of a trance, so try to get rid of anything that would draw you out of it. Take a moment to relax and settle in. Keep your hands at your sides and for a moment, don't *try* to do anything at all. Breathe. Let yourself go blank.

2. **Begin to focus.** Study the surface of the wall. Study it without a goal. You might find yourself focusing on its color or the patterns of light and dark or the texture of the surface. Keep your head in more or less the same position. (Limiting your field of vision in this way forces your mind to become more active and creative because it takes away your ability to create novelty by other means.) While keeping your body still, let your attention move freely to anything that it encounters within your limited field of vision.

3. **Unfocus.** Now let your eyes soften and blur a little so that motion and other effects can begin to enter your field of vision. It might help here to lean a little closer to the wall so that it's harder to focus your eyes. Try to let yourself see without seeing, the same way you do when you close your eyes and watch the patterns on the backs of your eyelids.

4. **Notice your mind at work.** You might start struggling with boredom here. Try to hang in there. It is in the mind's nature to seek change. What you're doing here is forcing your mind to *create* novelty with limited

input. Manufacturing mildly hallucinatory shapes and patterns is one way that it might do this. Or you may start to become hyperalert to sounds or smells. Whatever happens, it's likely that the solidity of the wall will dissolve a little bit. It will appear to take on slightly liquid characteristics. Keep staring at it until *something* happens. It doesn't matter what.

5. **Resolidify the wall.** Slowly move away from the wall, expanding your visual field. Do this one step at a time, pausing with each step to notice any changes as you move from a position of immersion in the wall to standing apart from it. Let yourself come back into the larger space. Breathe deeply. Finally, approach the wall again and put your palms on it. Experience it as a solid surface.

Boundaries and Barriers, Containment and Definition

What's the first association that comes into your mind when you think of the word *wall*? Is it a barrier? Is it a form of protection? A safe container or a prison? In their most basic function, walls mark boundaries, which is to say that they define things, are a form of language. Walls speak.

In therapy I often work with people who describe themselves as being "stuck." Often, when asked to create an image to go with the feeling of stuck-ness, they describe a wall. Sometimes they're evocative of famous cultural walls—the Great Wall of China, the Berlin Wall, the fence on the border between Mexico and the United States or between Israel and the West Bank. In exploring these images, the walls often first seem completely impenetrable. But inevitably, on closer examination, the walls will begin to evolve. This can happen in a myriad of ways. A wall can be scaled or tunneled. It may have secret doors and windows. It might become a holographic image that can be walked through.

We often think metaphorically of walls controlling us in some way. But as this exercise shows, we can co-create the meaning walls have in our lives by taking control of the perspective from which we see them.

Variations: Looking into the Void

Look closely at other things. You can probably remember the first time you ever stared closely at a photograph in a newspaper, how those microscopic dots metamorphosed into a natural-looking image. Staring at anything at close range alters your perception and challenges the assumption of solidity in the world. This exercise begins with a blank wall because there is an inherent absence of visual information in it. But you can expand the practice by following the same steps with other images and objects.

Start seeing walls. Some walls are obvious. But many natural and human-made objects actually function as walls even though they're not specifically intended as such. Look around, wherever you are, and divide everything you can see into two categories: wall and not wall. What happens if you think of everything in a particular space as a wall? What happens when you try to imagine the same place without any walls whatsoever?

Further Reading: Books on Walls and Fences

- Derry Brabbs, *Hadrian's Wall*, Frances Lincoln, 2008.
- Claire F. Fox, *The Fence and the River: Culture and Politics at the U.S.-Mexico Border*, University of Minnesota Press, 1999.
- Isabel Kershner, *Barrier: The Seam of the Israeli-Palestinian Conflict*, Palgrave Macmillan, 2005.
- Frederick Taylor, *The Berlin Wall: A World Divided, 1961–1989*, Harper Perennial, 2008.
- Michael Yamashita, *The Great Wall: From Beginning to End*, Sterling, 2007.

10

Catastrophize

You worry.

Of course you do. How could it be otherwise? You worry that you won't be able to do the things you're supposed to do ... or that you will do the things you're *not* supposed to. You worry that you'll let down the people who depend on you, and you worry that you'll be let down by people you depend on.

When you stop to think about it, you *know* that all this worrying is pointless. But it feels impossible to shut it off. You try to talk yourself out of it, telling yourself not to waste energy trying to manage things outside of your control. You try to force your mind to stop.

But it doesn't work.

Why not?

It's like that paradoxical instruction: don't think about a pink elephant.

Trying not to think about something only gives it more power.

This is why this exercise bypasses all that effort completely. Here, you will do precisely what every therapist in the world will tell you not to do: you will embrace and magnify a small worry until it expands into a catastrophic narrative in which your personal failings result in the end of the world as we know it. You might be surprised at how liberating apocalyptic fantasies can be.

What You'll Need
- A small but genuine worry

How to Do It
1. **Choose a worry.** What's on your to-do list right now? Pick something that will be a problem if you don't eventually get around to it . . . but that's not a matter of life or death right away. It could be changing the oil in your car, for instance, or backing up your computer's hard drive.
2. **Describe the task.** Do this in detail. Outline each step, from deciding on a time to get your oil changed and making an appointment at the shop to figuring out what you're going to do while the work is done. Then take a moment to imagine not doing each of these things, trying to kindle a bit of worry as you go.
3. **Find the loose thread that could lead to disaster.** This is where you really get down to some serious worrying. Project yourself into a future in which you

have failed to accomplish this task. What could happen as a result that would start you on the path to disaster? Keep it personal. You're on your way home from work when the Change Oil light suddenly goes on. The car stalls in the middle of the freeway, *all because you didn't change the oil.*

4. **Go global.** Now ask yourself: how could things get worse? What if, at that moment, your cell phone rings and it's your spouse, calling to tell you that your house is on fire, but you can't get home. Don't stop there. Find a way to let the crisis spread so that it's not just your own life you've screwed up but everyone else's as well. Can you construct a sequence of events in which your failure to change the oil in your car literally leads to world destruction?

5. **Restore the ordinary world.** As your mind fills with visions of mushroom clouds and nuclear winter, take a deep, cleansing breath. Look around the room. Feel its stability. It's not going away anytime soon. Think about your loved ones, where they are, and what they're doing at this moment. Imagine the moment when you will next see them. Feel gratitude for the ordinary world.

What's the Worst That Can Happen?

For those of us who are inclined to unnecessary worry (and I count myself among your number), this is an essential question, because what happens when you start worrying is that your perspective begins to contract. The thing you're worrying about suddenly becomes much larger in your mind than everything else. The best thing you can do for yourself when this happens is to find some way to widen your perspective. This simple question will do the trick, as long as you ask a few follow-up questions as well. If the worst that can happen is actually very bad, then ask yourself, "How likely is this outcome?" Usually the answer is reassuring. Next, ask yourself, "If it did happen, what would I do?" Again, usually you can come up with a pretty good answer. No matter what happens, you'll get through it.

Variations: Other Ways to Put Catastrophic Thinking to Use

Play God. Rather than being the victim of a catastrophe, be the perpetrator. Just in play, of course. This is a variation of every kid's favorite game: building a tower and then knocking it down. Get ahold of some children's toys—Legos, a dollhouse, or simple wooden blocks—and construct something from them. It could be an imitation of something from the real world or a simple tower. Then pretend there's an earthquake (or another disaster of your choice) and smash it all up. And when you feel like you're ready, add vengeance!

Imagine catastrophe as a new beginning. There's a reason that nearly every creation story in every culture contains a massive flood (or similar catastrophe) that purges the population and allows the creator to start anew. Within their destruction, catastrophes contain the paradoxical potential for renewal. Because they allow us to witness things that otherwise seem unimaginable (e.g., airplanes disappearing into a skyscraper, an entire American city under water), they are simultaneously both horrifying and fascinating. There is a purity in absolute destruction that can appeal to us in spite of all the horror, a possibility of deep renewal.

Link catastrophe and mindfulness. Fear, in small doses, sharpens our senses and brings us more fully into the present moment. Those who survive are able to make use of the fear they experience to guide their behavior in a constructive direction. Experiment with intentionally giving yourself *small* doses of fear and anxiety and then study how your body and mind react. How can you transform fear into a useful force in your life?

Further Reading: Books to Help You Imagine the Worst, Move Through It, and Move On

- *The Complete Manual of Things That Might Kill You: A Guide to Self-Diagnosis for Hypochondriacs*, Knock Knock Books, 2007.

- Gavin de Becker, *The Gift of Fear: Survival Signals that Protect Us from Violence*, Dell, 1997.
- Jon Kabat-Zinn, PhD, *Full Catastrophe Living: Using the Wisdom of Your Body and Mind to Face Stress, Pain, and Illness*, Delta, 1990.
- Joshua Piven and David Borgenicht, *The Complete Worst-Case Scenario Survival Handbook*, Chronicle Books, 2007.
- Amanda Ripley, *The Unthinkable: Who Survives When Disaster Strikes—and Why*, Three Rivers Press, 2009.
- Rebecca Solnit, *A Paradise Built in Hell: The Extraordinary Communities That Arise in Disasters*, Viking, 2009.
- Cameron Tuttle, *The Paranoid's Pocket Guide: Hundreds of Things You Never Knew You Had to Worry About*, Chronicle Books, 1997.

11

Let Your Mind Wander

You know the moment: you're sitting at work, supposedly editing a report, when you realize that instead of working you're making a mental catalog of all the dogs you've ever seen on television shows. How did your mind get onto this subject? You start tracing back the chain of associations. It started with Tiger, the dog on the *Brady Bunch*. You'd been thinking about the *Brady Bunch* because of a friend who is a parent in a blended family. You were thinking about your friend because he had recently asked you if his stepdaughter could do a job-shadow assignment with you for a day. The whole thing started because you had been imagining what it would be like to have someone observing you as you went about your workday.

What do you tell yourself when you emerge from such a trance? That you've been daydreaming? Wasting time? Or that you've been experiencing the spontaneous creative capacity of your own mind? I vote for the latter.

In this exercise you can reclaim the pleasure of free association by reversing the process, using a boring, repetitive activity to intentionally trigger spontaneous tangential thoughts. Can you catch yourself in the act of free associating? Is the thought that arises next intentional or unconscious? Can you tell the difference?

What You'll Need
- A boring mental task
- Pen and paper

How to Do It
1. **Pick a mental object to focus on.** The simplest option here is to use a mantra. Try making it an impenetrable legalistic phrase (say, "reference the aforementioned precedent"). Or if you're studying a foreign language, you might give yourself a sequence of vocabulary words to learn. Or make a pointless list to memorize—brands of cars, names of senators, types of vegetables, and so on.
2. **Go to work.** Repeat the mantra, memorize the list, or whatever. Observe yourself as you do. Sooner or later (probably sooner), your mind will wander. The moment you realize this has happened, stop and write down the thought that interrupted you. It's possible (even likely) that you won't catch yourself right away. In this case,

track it back and write down the series of associative thoughts that got your mind where it is.

3. **Let your mind wander.** If you're the disciplined type, you might find this step difficult. Your impulse will be to return diligently to the pointless task. Don't let yourself do that. Instead, read aloud what you've just written. Then take a breath, let your mind go blank, and see what comes into it. Your obedient mind might continue to get in the way here with worries about how you're spending your time or whether you're doing the exercise correctly. Gently ask this part of yourself to step aside. Wait until a genuinely independent thought arises. When it does, write it down. If that thought leads somewhere else, follow it, letting your thoughts flow as freely as possible, writing down everything as best you can.

4. **Repeat.** Some people will be able to spend hours on step 3. If you're one of them, take ten minutes or so to enjoy the associative ride, and then move on to step 5. But for many people there will eventually come a pause in your thoughts. When this happens, take another breath and return to the mental task you started with, and then begin the process again.

5. **Return to linearity.** In the course of doing this exercise, you've let yourself get a little loose around the edges. It won't do to send you out into the world spouting non sequiturs. So before you return to your

regular life, take a moment to reconstitute your linear self. Do this by making a very serious face and saying something that sounds presidential. Then give your head and arms a good shake and go about your business.

Creating Creativity

The great paradox of creativity is that it is very difficult to arrive at it intentionally. And yet, as this exercise demonstrates, we are all constantly (if secretly) manifesting our ability to think in a nonlinear fashion. For the most part, we're rewarded for keeping ourselves "inside the box." I don't care how much we may talk about being "outside" that box; we rarely allow ourselves the opportunity to revel in our own capacity for open-ended creativity and absurdity. We instinctively know that creativity is invigorating and that play is restorative. But we refrain from practicing either one. Why? Because creativity is scary. It's messy. It contains an element of anarchy. The deep message within any creative act is always this: things can be different.

Yes, that's what I'm telling you: daydreaming can be a revolutionary act.

Variations: Other Ways to Let Your Mind Wander

Simple daydreaming. Although the line between free association and daydreaming sometimes blurs, they are in fact different activities. Daydreaming is an act of fantasy, and daydreams have a certain narrative coherence. Free association, in its strictest sense, has no such coherence. Try doing this exercise substituting a dreamy fantasy for random associations. What story emerges?

Read *Finnegans Wake.* James Joyce's impenetrable classic is surely the most deeply free-associative literary work of all time. It's just intelligible enough to make you feel like you should be able understand it, but every phrase simultaneously unravels into incoherence. Let it loosen your mind with sentences like this: "Fudder and lighting for ally looty, any filly in a fog, for O'Cronione lags acrumbling in his sands but his sunsunsuns still tumble on" (1971, 415).

Impose onerous restrictions. In this exercise the boring mental task is used as something for your creative mind to rebel against. You can up the ante by briefly imposing more draconian requirements. For instance, try doing the exercise with a meaningless censorship on yourself (say, no thoughts about food!). Chances are good that your mind will rebel and your free associations will be all the richer.

Play. It's as simple as it gets. Find a four-year-old (other ages are okay, too, but four is particularly great) and follow his or her lead.

Further Reading: Books on Free Association, Play, and Creativity

- Diane Ackerman, *Deep Play*, Vintage Books, 1999.
- Stuart Brown, MD, with Christopher Vaughan, *Play: How It Shapes the Brain, Opens the Imagination, and Invigorates the Soul*, Avery, 2009.
- James Joyce, *Finnegans Wake*, Viking, 1971.
- Stephen Nachmanovitch, *Free Play: Improvisation in Life and Art*, J. P. Tarcher, 1990.

12

Lie to Yourself

You know that one really, really good friend you've got? The one who is *such* a good friend that he or she calls you out when you get full of it? We all have blind spots, but what if it were possible to rise above our own perceptions, to be ourselves and simultaneously be that friend to ourselves? Try it. Spend a few minutes engaging in a piece of wishful thinking, walking the line between fantasy and reality. Can you hold both in mind at once?

What You'll Need
• Something you wish were true that you know is not

How to Do It
1. **Choose a piece of wishful thinking.** Identify some small lie that you tell yourself on a regular basis. Maybe you pretend that you're confident when you're really quite shy. Maybe you tell yourself you weigh less than you do. Or maybe you lie to yourself about the future,

telling yourself that an investment you made is going to pay off big-time.

2. **Anchor the fantasy.** What if it were true? Take a few minutes to imagine what that would be like. Get concrete and get expansive. What exactly would have to happen, for instance, for that sketchy company you invested in to hit it big? Did it just sign a deal to supply a key widget that Apple will use in its next-generation iPod? Whatever it is, feel it as if it were the truth.

3. **Count your chickens.** Your mind will probably start doing this even without your trying to make it happen. But give it a push. In your imagination, start making the extreme changes that are the result of your fantasy coming true. Buy a new house. Get married . . . or divorced! Buy a private jet. Move to Paris or wherever your mind may take you.

4. **Notice yourself.** Close your eyes and notice the effect that these fantasies are having on your physical being. Is your heart racing? Are your hands clammy? How's your breathing?

5. **Come back to reality.** Do this gently, without judgment of any kind. Open your eyes and look around the room. Look at your body. Really take it all in. This is your life. Then reexamine your fantasy in all its splendor. This is your aspiration. You exist somewhere between the two. See if you can simultaneously hold

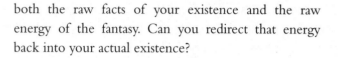

both the raw facts of your existence and the raw energy of the fantasy. Can you redirect that energy back into your actual existence?

Lies, Aspirations, and Creative Visualization: A Tangled Web

Where is the line between harmful self-deception and constructive affirmation? If you've done this exercise correctly (and, of course, it's impossible to do it incorrectly), you might be experiencing some confusion about this question. When Stuart Smalley looks in the mirror and starts his spiel—"I'm good enough, I'm smart enough . . ."—we laugh *and* we wince because we feel the gap between the desire and the reality. We recognize both that he's lying to himself and that he's aspiring to the best in himself. And, of course, we know all too well what it's like to be free-floating in the void between what we wish were true about ourselves and what we know we really are.

But here's the exciting secret behind this exercise: the void is cool! Really. The gap we create when we fantasize or even outright lie to ourselves is energizing and enlivening and gives us essential forward momentum. It's only a problem because our brains are wired to resist states of uncertainty. We want to anchor ourselves to a clear and certain thing, whether it's fantasy or reality, the past or the

future. But the void is a place of uncertainty; it's the gap between the poles, where all things are possible. It is, in fact, the present moment.

Variations: Affirm Yourself

Extreme affirmations. I probably shouldn't admit this, but I've always struggled with affirmations. I can never do them with a straight face. If you're like me in this way, you can try tricking yourself into experiencing some of the benefits of affirmations by taking them to absurd extremes. In this technique, I highly recommend the use of quotes from Muhammad Ali:

> "I am the greatest; I said that even before I knew I was."
> "Superman don't need no seat belt."
> "When you are as great as I am, it is hard to be humble."

Anti-affirmations. This is another technique for those of you who are skeptical of affirmations. In this case, rather than building yourself up absurdly, you tear yourself down with statements that are so extreme that they can't possibly be true. Here, I recommend starting with lines from Rodney Dangerfield:

> "I was so ugly my mother used to feed me with a slingshot."

"When I was born, I was so ugly the doctor slapped my mother."

"I'm a bad lover. I once caught a Peeping Tom booing me."

Write yourself into a rap song. Find the most outrageously boastful rap song you can, the one that describes a reality that is ridiculously unlike your own life. Learn the song, writing in variations that refer specifically to you. Sing it in the shower.

Further Reading: Books on Lying and Self-Deception

- Robert Burton, MD, *On Being Certain: Believing You Are Right Even When You're Not*, St. Martin's Press, 2008.
- Paul Ekman, *Telling Lies: Clues to Deceit in the Marketplace, Politics, and Marriage*, W. W. Norton, 2009.
- Cordelia Fine, *A Mind of Its Own: How Your Brain Distorts and Deceives*, W. W. Norton, 2008.
- Chris Frith, *Making Up the Mind: How the Brain Creates Our Mental World*, Blackwell Publishing, 2007.

13

Do Something

But what?

If you're looking to send yourself into a complete tailspin of uncertainty, there's nothing quite like the experience of *absolute freedom*. Now, don't get me wrong; the point of this exercise is not to give you an anxiety attack, nor is it intended to help you get anything done. The goal here is for you to experience as fully as possible the universe of possible actions, and to open yourself to a full awareness of the "pause" between inaction and action, because it's that pause that makes everything possible.

What You'll Need
- Nothing

How to Do It
1. **Make a list.** Start making a mental list of everything that you could possibly do right at this moment. Don't try to write it down; don't try to remember any of it.

Just start listing things, out loud if you want, as fast as you can. I could ride my bike. I could cover my ears. I could whistle. The possibilities are obviously endless. Keep them that way.

2. **Keep listing.** After a few minutes of this, you're going to start wanting some sense of resolution, either by stopping the activity or by making a choice and actually doing something. Or you might have the impulse to think about the associations that have arisen as you made your list. Resist these temptations as best you can. Try to keep expanding your list, even when it feels like you can't go on.

3. **Empty your mind.** When you feel like you really can't keep going, allow yourself to stop listing. Take a slow breath. See if, after the rush of mental activity that you've manipulated yourself into, you can let your mind go completely blank. At this point there's a good chance that your mind is going to have a hard time stopping and that more possibilities for action will keep coming to you. Don't worry. Let your mind do what it will. Just try not to make it do anything in particular.

4. **Wait.** Feel the ridiculously large range of possible actions before you, and take a moment to choose none of them. If your mind pushes you toward action, get defiant about it—refuse to act.

5. Imagine a choice. Finally, allow one last possible action to come into your mind. Don't worry about what it is and don't censor it in any way. Let it be mundane, random, constructive, absurd ... whatever. Now take a minute or two to imagine doing this one particular thing and this thing only. Start by holding the awareness of everything that you are *not* doing by choosing this single option. All of those many, many possible things you imagined (not to mention the thousands of other things that you didn't have time to list) are going undone as you focus single-mindedly on this one action. When you are ready, take a deep breath and go on with your day, feeling free to actually do the thing you have been imagining ... or not.

Zen and the Art of Waffling

This exercise combines two important strands in the history of human consciousness: our existential awareness of an emptiness at the center of our beings and our inexhaustible capacity for indecision. We are all driven, to a greater or a lesser degree, by a powerful cultural pressure to perform, achieve, and show tangible progress as we move forward through our lives. Get a degree! Get a promotion! Write a book! And we are all—again, to a greater or lesser degree—stymied by the difficulties and complications of these choices, brought about by the combination of the

range of options before us and the possibility of making the wrong choice.

I think that's why many people—myself included—easily become overwhelmed when trying to understand the core concepts of Buddhism. Buddhism says that it's all emptiness. Life is just a web of mental activity woven around an empty center, giving the false impression of solidity to our existence. The classic way to begin to understand this truth is, of course, mindfulness meditation. But as this exercise should show, a path to this awareness is available to us at every moment in our everyday lives. Bringing awareness to the infinite choices within the simple act of "doing something" can open us to an invigorating experience of the emptiness at the center of our being.

Variations: Infinite Possibilities

Do something *different.* This exercise is a version of a well-known psychotherapeutic technique in which the therapist simply instructs the patient to take a habitual unhelpful behavior and "do something different." Try modifying this exercise by adding the word *different* to it, imagining each of your possible actions done differently or focusing on a single action and imagining endless variations on how it could be done.

Actually do something. What would it be like if you actually tried to do everything that is possible to do?

Try it and find out. Take a few minutes to generate a list of possible activities and then actually try to do them.

Further Reading: Books on Action and Inaction, Emptiness, and Zen

- Sylvia Boorstein, *Don't Just Do Something, Sit There: A Mindfulness Retreat with Sylvia Boorstein*, HarperOne, 1996.
- Guy Newland, *Introduction to Emptiness: As Taught in Tsong-Kha-Pa's Great Treatise on the Stages of the Path*, Snow Lion Publications, 2008.
- Shunryu Suzuki, *Zen Mind, Beginner's Mind*, Shambhala, 2006.
- Alan W. Watts, *The Way of Zen*, Vintage Books, 1989.

14

Lust

Sounds fun, right? At first, at least. But things get complicated really fast. For the purposes of this exercise, try to separate lust from the concept of "sin." And try not to limit it to sex either. Think of lust as simple, amorphous energy. It can be used for good or for evil. An orgy is an expression of lust, and so is a nuclear bomb. The Olympics are an expression of lust, and so is a cock fight. Lust is the raw, hungry desire that moves the world forward, even as it can threaten its very existence. Can you let yourself draw on its energy without tipping over into self-destruction?

What You'll Need
• An unfulfilled desire

How to Do It
1. **Choose an object of desire.** While lust is commonly equated with sex, don't limit yourself to sexual fantasies.

Consider the thousand-dollar dinner in New York's fanciest restaurant, a sip from a ten-thousand-dollar bottle of wine, or a billion dollars in your bank account. Keep in mind that everyone is different in relationship to lust. For some, lust comes easily ... even a little too easily. Others are limited in their capacity for lust because desire itself feels taboo. You're probably somewhere in the middle. Remember that what you choose doesn't have to look like the textbook definition of lust to anyone else. It just has to feel like lust to you.

2. **Elaborate the fantasy.** Make it specific and detailed. Include all the senses. And cast it as a narrative: Where did it start? Where is it going? Close your eyes and let yourself sink into the details.

3. **Surrender to the fantasy.** Why is it that very famous people so often get caught with their pants down (so to speak) in compromising situations? It's partly about fame itself, of course, but I think it has even more to do with the nature of lust. It's a powerful force, deeply programmed within us, that has the ability to override reason. But no matter how powerful the urge toward lust may feel, there is always a moment of choice in which a person *decides* to give himself or herself over to desire. Make that moment explicit, remembering that this is purely fantasy. Choose to surrender to your desire.

4. Resist resolution. The standard narrative of lust begins with a heightening of desire and concludes with the dissipation of that desire in a moment of orgasmic release. But in this fantasy, imagine that your lust is inexhaustible. No orgasm can quell your desire; no food can satiate your appetite. And that's okay because this is a fantasy of deep abundance. As your lust increases, there is always more of what you desire before you.

5. Ride the energy. Gradually bring yourself back into the present moment, letting yourself feel the whirl of raw lusty energy still in your body. Just feel it for what it is—energy—and see if you can ride that energy as you move forward through the rest of your day, like a surfer on a powerful wave.

Controlled from Beyond

We sometimes experience lust as a force beyond our conscious control. And it's always a little spooky to feel like we're being controlled by forces beyond our awareness. No one was very happy, for instance, when Sigmund Freud first proposed the existence of the unconscious. While few people today would seriously argue against its existence, we've come to understand many other ways in which our behavior is influenced by forces beyond our conscious intention. For instance, Stanley Milgram's classic experiments demonstrated that most of us can be

manipulated into violating our own moral code when we believe that we are obliged to obey authority. In those experiments (done in the early sixties), Milgram gave his subjects the task of "teaching" another subject (actually a confederate of the researcher) a simple memory task. The teacher's job was to administer a shock to the learner, who was hidden behind a wall, for each wrong answer given, with the shock gradually increasing in voltage for repeated mistakes. In fact, there was no shock—just the sound of a shock followed by recorded sounds of cries and then the screams of the learner. Though many teachers were uncomfortable doing so, in the end 65 percent of them gave their learner a 450-volt shock. The teachers weren't bad people; they weren't sociopaths. They were simply demonstrating an unfortunate human trait: under the right conditions, our behavior can be powerfully controlled by forces outside our conscious control.

Many of these sorts of unconscious influences can, with effort, be brought into our conscious awareness. But evolutionary psychologists are also arguing quite persuasively that there is a set of powerful genetic forces operating within all of us beneath the level of conscious intention. According to this argument, all of our behavior is driven by the underlying reality that our genes are evolutionarily designed solely to reproduce themselves ruthlessly.

Where does lust fit in for you on this spectrum? Is it a force that you feel as a part of yourself? Or is it hidden behind a veil? Or is it somewhere in between?

Variations: More Experiments with the Energy of Lust

Desire the undesirable. Turn this exercise on its head and see if you can detach the experience of desire from desirable objects themselves. Start by letting yourself feel the intense desire that you experienced in the original exercise. Then swap the object of your attention for something you find neutral, unpleasant, or even disgusting. Can you hold the feeling of desire even while you contemplate the image of something distasteful?

Remote control. Schizophrenics sometimes experience a frightening phenomenon known as "delusions of control," in which they feel that their thoughts and actions are under the control of some external person, group, or force. The experience of lust can be sort of like that, seeming to take over the conscious mind from the outside. Let yourself imagine that this is actually true, that some outside force—aliens, the CIA, your Bible study group—is controlling your experience of desire. How does imagining that it is not under your own control change the experience of lust?

Try being a porn star. Just in your imagination. Porn stars have become symbols of pure lust, and for

obvious reasons: there they are, having lots and lots of sex, with lots and lots of different people. But is this lust? Is the reputation deserved? It's a matter of debate. Come to an informed decision on this question by allowing yourself to imaginatively explore what your life would be like as a porn actor. Make it as vivid as you can. Don't just jump to the sex. Make sure to think about how you'd get hired, the mechanics of the set, hygiene, personal relationships, and collecting your paycheck.

Plan a bank robbery. Just as porn stars are symbols of sexual lust, bank robbers are symbols of lust for wealth. And just as being a porn actor doesn't actually seem like the most effective way to satisfy sexual lust, bank robbery strikes me as one of the least sensible ways to act out an uncontrollable lust for money. Still, the *fantasy* makes sense—all that money is there in one place. Let yourself plan a bank robbery in as much detail as your noncriminal mind will allow. Does doing this increase the lust, or does it drain it all away?

Further Reading: Books on Evolutionary Psychology and Authoritarianism

- Ori Brafman and Rom Brafman, *Sway: The Irresistible Pull of Irrational Behavior*, Doubleday, 2008.

- David Buss, *Evolutionary Psychology: The New Science of the Mind*, Allyn & Bacon, 2007.
- Richard Dawkins, *The Selfish Gene*, Oxford University Press, 2006.
- Stanley Milgram, *Obedience to Authority: An Experimental View*, Harper & Row, 1974.

15

Have a Drink

I'll tell you what you *don't* need. You don't need one more person telling you that you should drink more water. Of course you should. It's good for you. But you already know that, and like so many things that are good for you, after you've been told to do it four thousand times, you tend to stop listening. So this is not an exercise aimed at getting you to drink more water. The point here is to reexperience the ordinary *act* of drinking as an elemental physical experience. After that, go ahead and drink as much or as little water as you feel like. It's entirely up to you.

What You'll Need
- Water
- A container

How to Do It
1. **Choose a container.** It sounds simple, but this first step marks a choice that will fundamentally define the

rest of the exercise. The experience of drinking from a mug is very different than that of drinking from a wine glass. And it's miles away from drinking out of a baby bottle. Let yourself consider the huge range of drinking vessels available to you: jam jars, bowls, straws, your cupped hands, and so on. While you're at it, choose a source for your water—still or sparkling, tap or filtered.

2. **Sip.** Begin by connecting your lips to the liquid in your chosen container. Raise the container to your lips, or lower your lips to the container (it doesn't matter which). Before you let any of the liquid enter your mouth, feel the sensation of the water against your lips. Notice not just the sensation of wetness but also the quality of pressure that is inherent in the water. Then, when you're ready, open your mouth gently and let a small sip spill into your mouth.

3. **Swirl.** Hold the water there for a moment. Feel how it affects the inside of your mouth to have this new liquid inside it. If you can, notice how holding water in your mouth also changes the way you experience the rest of your body. After a moment, you'll probably find that the impulse to swallow will grow quite strong. Try to resist this urge for now. Move the water into different areas of your mouth. How does it feel near the tip of your tongue and the back of your lips? How is it different

when you let it pour into the sides of your cheeks, or when you let it rest near the back of your palate?

4. **Swallow.** Because swallowing is a reflex, it can be difficult to swallow mindfully. Try to notice the shifts in the front part of your mouth and the tightening in the throat that moves the liquid into "swallowing position." Then feel the esophageal clench that pushes the water down into your stomach. Feel it in your Adam's apple. Try to be aware of the sensation of the liquid moving down into your stomach. There's a tremendous amount going on, so feel free to do repeated experiments with this step, trying to become increasingly aware of the intricate mechanics of swallowing.

5. **Say "aaaaah."** Drinking is refreshing. So yes, as a closing ritual to this exercise, I want you to lean your head back and open your mouth so that you feel the full openness of your moistened throat. Then say a good, loud "aaaaah" as if you were an actor in a soft drink commercial.

An Aside: The Worst-Tasting Thing I've Ever Drunk

Not long ago I was suffering from some vague medical problems that my doctors had been unable to diagnose. So when someone recommended that I see a Chinese herbalist, I was willing to give it a try. I wandered into the Chinese herbal pharmacy and sat down with the herbalist, who was feeling people's pulses and writing out prescriptions in the back of the store. He put his fingers on my wrists and assessed my pulse as I explained my symptoms to him as best I could through a Cantonese interpreter. He nodded, smiled, and then told me that my liver had too much heat. He wrote out a prescription and handed it to the interpreter, and suddenly a rush of activity coalesced behind the pharmacy's long counter as a small crew of workers laid out seven paper plates and started placing little piles of brown, black, and white objects on each plate. "Mostly tree bark," the interpreter told me when I asked what they were. "Some mushrooms, some seeds." She explained, as they poured the contents of each plate into a paper bag, that after dinner each night for a week I should boil the contents of one of the bags for an hour and then let it cool and drink it down.

That sounded fine to me.

But when the herbs started to boil that first night, I began to realize what I was in for. The entire house became infused with a bitter smell that had no corollary in my routine vocabulary of taste and smell. It smelled crude and ancient and a little rotten. It smelled the way it feels when a fairy-tale figure gets lost in the woods.

I boiled it down until there was less than a cup's worth of the dark brown brew. I strained it, poured it into a mug, and then stared at it as I watched it cool. My wife

got the camera out, hardly able to believe that I was actually going to be able to drink this bitter brew. I could hardly believe it either. I wasn't sure that I could get it down without gagging. But I relaxed my throat and let the liquid in, gulping the entire thing down fast, letting the sharp tannins abrade my mouth and tongue, my throat, and even my stomach. I shook with the intensity of the sensation, took a deep breath, and then slowly regulated my body and my breathing back to normal.

Variations: Drinking Games

Gulp. Try taking the exercise in exactly the opposite direction by speeding things up and trying to gulp mindfully. This is, of course, a contradiction in terms. But that doesn't make it any less useful. Gulping minimizes the experience of tasting. It's entirely focused on quickly getting liquids into our bodies. And sometimes that is exactly what we need to do.

Spit. This is yet another way to work against the original premise of this exercise. Spitting is related to gagging and vomiting—it's a reflex designed to expel unwanted materials from our bodies. It's considered socially unacceptable, of course, but it's still an elemental human activity, and it's at least as mechanically complex as drinking is.

Experiment with stimulants. This is an advanced exercise, so please proceed with caution. By stimulants, I mean anything stronger than water—juices, carbonated beverages, caffeinated drinks (both hot and cold), and of course, alcoholic beverages. Finally, I would add unpleasant-tasting liquids to the list, as in my description of Chinese herbal tea. Each of these adds different levels of complexity to the experience of drinking, some to do with the physical sensation of the liquid, some to do with the effects of the liquid on our bodies. Remember that the point is not to alter your state as a result of drinking, but to alter your awareness of the act of drinking itself.

Further Reading: Books for Those Who Want Someone to Tell Them to Drink More Water

- F. Batmanghelidj, MD, *Water for Health, for Healing, for Life: You're Not Sick, You're Thirsty!* Warner Books, 2003.
- Masaru Emoto, *The Hidden Messages in Water,* Beyond Words Publishing, 2004.
- Steve Meyerowitz, *Water: The Ultimate Cure: Discover Why Water Is the Most Important Ingredient in Your Diet and Find Out Which Water Is Right for You,* Sproutman Publications, 2000.
- Christopher Vasey, ND, *The Water Prescription: For Health, Vitality, and Rejuvenation,* Healing Arts Press, 2006.

Misuse an Object

Remember how, in those old Betty Boop cartoons, ordinary objects could suddenly take on lives of their own? A face emerged on a fork and started to salivate. A car raced along and then stood up and paused to take a series of deep breaths. We think of physical objects as fixed things, but there's no need to bind ourselves to this assumption. Break through to the hidden life of the material world by intentionally misusing a familiar object. Change the world by altering your perceptions.

What You'll Need
• A common object

How to Do It
1. **Choose an object.** Anything will do. Really.
2. **See the object anew.** This is the visual equivalent of repeating a word or a phrase so many times that it starts

to sound completely bizarre. Imagine that you have never seen this object before and that you can't possibly imagine what it's for. This is the heart of the exercise, and it's the hardest step, because it asks you to force your practical mind into an imaginative mode. (Hint: if there is a child nearby, ask for assistance; kids are much better at this sort of thing than adults are.)

3. **Tell the object's creation story.** Now that you have (at least partly) stopped seeing the object in the way that it was intended to be seen, try to come up with a creation story for why it exists. Think about traditional stories that explain why things are the way they are, like how the zebra got its stripes or why the elephant has a trunk. Think of your object as if you are Adam in the Garden of Eden, as if you'd just come across it and you have to come up with a justification for its existence.

4. **Rename the object.** Sticking with the Garden of Eden theme, assign yourself the task of naming this strange new object. There are many approaches to this. You might make up entirely new words. You might take the names of several already-existing objects and combine them into a new name. Or you might come up with a long and overly literal description of the purpose you are going to put it to. Again, children are helpful here. If you know any, ask them for help.

5. **Put it to use.** Whatever you have decided on as the purpose for the object, use it that way now. With any luck, the purpose that you have defined will be so ridiculous that trying to use it that way will feel delightfully absurd. But whatever the outcome, don't allow yourself to be frustrated by a sense of ridiculousness. Know, in fact, that if you feel completely ridiculous, you've done the exercise just right.

Psychedelic, Man!

Human beings have a long history of using mind-altering substances not just to numb themselves from harsh realities, but also to open their minds into new and expansive ways of perceiving the reality that we have come to take as a solid thing that's well defined, a given. Not that I'm advocating the use of psychedelic drugs here; quite the opposite, in fact. This exercise is meant to allow us a small opening into our mind's natural capacity for psychedelic thinking and perception. When we loosen (just a little) the concept of fixed meanings, we open the possibility of redefining not just our own experience but the actual definition of the physical world we inhabit.

Variations: Inventing the World

Creation stories. The reason these sorts of stories remain so powerful is that they briefly allow us to undo our fixed explanations about why things are the way they are. They allow us to shift into a state of mind in which meaning itself is up for grabs. You can expand this exercise by making up creation stories for everything you see around you. When doing this, try to detach from the literal world as much as possible. Become fantastic and ridiculous.

Look-alikes. I don't know of anyone who better embodies the skills of this exercise than Joan Steiner in her seemingly endless series of books in which ordinary objects are misused to create the illusion of other objects. Expand this exercise by using an object (or objects) to create other familiar objects.

Invent. Inventors amaze me. I don't have the sort of mind that can create something completely out of nothing. My mind struggles to see a function that could be filled by an object that has yet to be created. The misuse of common objects as done in this exercise can be seen as a stepping stone to the creation of new objects. Try your hand at invention. Or go online and check out the U.S. Patent and Trademark Office (www.uspto.gov) and amaze yourself with what other people are thinking up.

Further Reading: Creation Stories, Look-Alikes, Psychedelics, and Animation

- Richard Fleischer, *Out of the Inkwell: Max Fleischer and the Animation Revolution*, University Press of Kentucky, 2005.

 **ANDREW PETERSON**

- Aldous Huxley, *The Doors of Perception and Heaven and Hell*, Perennial Classics, 2004.
- Barbara C. Sproul, *Primal Myths: Creating the World*, Harper & Row, 1979.
- Joan Steiner, *Look-Alikes: The More You Look, the More You See!* Little, Brown, 2003.

17

Retrieve an Item from the Trash

Becoming more mindful about the waste you produce is an important step in changing your environmental habits. That's not the goal of this exercise (although it may be a side effect). Here you will run exercise 6, Throw Something Away, in reverse. Push the rewind button on your life: reclaim an object from the trash and attempt to bring it back to life.

What You'll Need
• Object from your trash can

How to Do It
1. **Pick an object from the trash.** Ideally, this would be the last thing that you've thrown away. That keeps the exercise as random as possible. Realistically, though, it's okay to exercise a bit of discretion in making this choice. Start by deciding which trash can to choose from. You might consider using one from an office rather than the

kitchen to minimize your involvement with organic matter, which is not the optimal material for this exercise. The object you choose could be something that has been altered in the process of discarding it (shredded or crumpled paper; a flattened tin can), or it could be something that is simply used up (an empty shampoo bottle), or it could be anything in between.

2. **Contemplate the object's history.** Holding the object before you, narrate the story of its life. Do this as if it is your child (an adopted child, really). Imagine it's her birthday and that you're telling her the story of how she came into your life. Make up the object's history if you don't know it. If you're looking at a crumpled up piece of paper, for instance, you might start by imagining the newspapers that were recycled to create her. Then move on to the trip to the office supply store, where you bought the ream she came from, and how she sat in the middle of the ream for days and weeks until finally it was her turn to go through the printer. And what should happen but a paper jam! She was crumpled up and thrown away, never imagining that she was to return again.

3. **Contemplate the object's future as an item of trash.** If you hadn't stepped in to alter the object's destiny, where would it have gone? Picture the object inside a garbage bag, taken out to the can in the alley, picked up by

the truck, compacted, and then dumped in the landfill. Try to imagine it, crushed together with everything else inside the bag, slowly, slowly decomposing.

4. **Rewind.** As best you can, reverse the steps that led you to dispose of the object in the first place. Some objects will be easier than others in this regard, so you might have to get creative. It's easy enough to smooth out a crumpled-up piece of paper, for instance. But there's no way to run it in reverse through the printer. Get metaphorical, if you'd like, as you symbolically give the object a new birth.

5. **Give it a fresh start.** Finally, find a way to reuse the object. You can do this in one of two ways. The first is practical: how could this object find a useful purpose in the world in its newly restored form? (Don't limit yourself to its original uses here. Try to think creatively about its potential uses.) Second—and this is much more fun— consider the object as an element in an artistic creation. What sort of artistic project could you create using this object? Once you've decided on a way to reuse the object, don't act on your decision. Simply set the object aside, go about your business, and notice over the next days and weeks if and how the object reenters your awareness.

Garbage as a Transitional Object

You are probably familiar with the concept of the transitional object. These are the physical objects that children

use to help themselves cope emotionally with separation from their parents. The child gets out of bed, takes his stuffed raccoon to his mother, and insists that she give it a kiss. She kisses it, and suddenly it is covered with what developmental psychologists like to call "mommy dust." The child toddles off to bed, clutching the newly recharged raccoon, and he is able to fall asleep. The object forms an emotional bridge between the child and parent, allowing him to feel secure in his awareness that he will be reunited with his mother when he wakes.

So what does this have to do with garbage?

Garbage contains objects from our material culture. We may not be aware of it, but we have an intimate relationship to all of it. The material objects that surround us help us know and remember who we are. And these relationships are undergoing constant separations. Garbage is the most concrete representation of this process. The trash can is a portal. In terms of the scene just described, in this exercise you are letting a piece of trash make one last trip back to you before it shuts its eyes and goes to sleep.

Variations: Act Out Your Issues in Your Relationship with Trash

Go into denial. That's to say, don't let yourself throw anything away. Throwing something away is like sending it to its death, so take a little time to pretend that death doesn't exist. For a limited period of time (a day or so is good), keep everything that you would ordinarily throw away. Don't put it away; that defeats the purpose. Just let it accumulate on counters and the floor, wherever you have space.

Get clingy. Take the previous paragraph to a higher level by refusing to let your trash out of your sight. (This is a hard practice to maintain for more than a few minutes.)

Act all superior. Try to make your trash feel bad by acting like you simply don't care about it. Refuse to acknowledge that it has any meaning at all in your life.

Further Reading: Books on Our Relationships with Objects

- Josh Glenn and Carol Hayes, *Taking Things Seriously: 75 Objects with Unexpected Significance*, Princeton Architectural Press, 2007.
- Daniel Miller, *The Comfort of Things*, Polity, 2008.
- John C. Ryan and Alan Thein Durning, *Stuff: The Secret Lives of Everyday Things*, Northwest Environment Watch, 1997.
- Sherry Turkle, ed., *Evocative Objects: Things We Think With*, MIT Press, 2007.

18

Give It All Away

It sounds scary, I know. So you should know from the start that you're not *actually* going to give away anything in this exercise. You're just going to try to convince yourself for a few minutes that you are capable of letting go of something that you truly believe you can't live without. Let yourself briefly experience the anxiety of loss; then see if you can catch a quick glimpse of the freedom that lies on the other side.

What You'll Need
• Awareness of the things you're most attached to

How to Do It
1. **Identify the thing that you most feel you could not live without.** Take your time with this first step, because the depth of your attachment is what will drive the rest of the exercise. Consider a big thing like your salary or your house. It could also be more conceptual—

your personal power or material wealth, your dignity or your sense of safety. It could even be a relationship.

2. **Cling.** Start by intensifying your attachment to whatever you've chosen. Describe to yourself how badly you need this thing in your life. Identify with it, as if it were part of the very cellular structure of your being. Convince yourself that you will *die* without it—literally die.

3. **Imagine being forced to give it up.** Since you are not naturally going to want to give up this cherished thing voluntarily, begin by imagining a villain wresting it away from you. Maybe it's the bank foreclosing on your house. Maybe it's someone kidnapping your children. Whatever it is, you should start to feel some resistance here. You're working against your own basic human nature.

4. **Give it away voluntarily.** Having let yourself imagine this most essential thing *taken away* from you, can you now imagine giving it away voluntarily? This step asks you to make a truly illogical leap, so you might have to create an elaborate narrative to hold it. What would lead you to voluntarily give your own child away? Could you do it, for instance, if you were Tibetan and you were informed that he had been identified as the next incarnation of the Dalai Lama? Breathe deeply and let go.

5. **Who are you without it?** Now feel yourself in the absence of this most essential thing. Imagine your life

without it. How would you move forward? You have just convinced yourself that you will die without it, so perhaps what you'll experience now is a sort of death. If so, let it be. Just sit quietly without trying to control your thoughts. Let your mind struggle with the loss. You may find yourself moving through the familiar stages of grief. If so, stay with it until your mind stops struggling and starts to settle. Whatever you discover at that moment will be your gift.

Giving Away, Letting Go

This exercise magnifies a simple truth of our existence: everything that we have can go away at any moment. That reality can be so difficult to comprehend. I was reawakened to it while I was volunteering in Louisiana in the days shortly after Katrina hit. The sentence I heard most often was simply this: "We lost *everything*."

I struggled, then and still, to grasp that. It can happen. We can lose everything at any moment. There's nothing we can do to change that.

But, of course, there is something that you can't lose, something that can't be taken away from you, and that is your ability to choose your attitude toward that loss.

This brings us to Viktor Frankl. His story about the survival of the soul in the face of the brutal reality of Auschwitz, told in his book *Man's Search for Meaning*, is widely known, but I still find myself telling it to my patients regularly. If you haven't read the book already, you must. If you have read it before, you need to read it again. We all do. Because Frankl was able to glimpse an elemental human truth within the horrific circumstances of a Nazi concentration camp: everything can be taken from us *except* for the ability to choose our attitude toward our life. Understanding that changes everything.

Variations: Give and Take

Explore *actual* **giving.** You do it all the time, of course. But how mindful are you when you do it, whether you're giving a bit of your ice cream to your child or handing a dollar bill to a beggar on the street? True giving inevitably includes an experience of loss, but we tend to shield ourselves from this reality either by idealizing our giving ("I am selfless!") or by denying the significance of what we give ("I don't care that much about it anyway."). Try experimenting with mindful giving by making yourself aware of the full range of your emotional experience in the many small moments of giving that take place in your day-to-day life.

Imagine *taking.* In order to more deeply understand what it means to give, try reversing the whole direction of the exercise. Imagine yourself taking the things that matter most from someone else. You may need to temporarily

adopt the persona of an evil villain to do this because there's a sadism in this sort of taking that (fortunately) doesn't come easily to most of us. But it is always instructive to try to understand the points of view of others, even (perhaps especially) when they seem to be evil.

Consider deprivation. It's not easy to imagine yourself relinquishing the things that most define you. In doing this exercise, many people will get in touch with strong feelings of deprivation. What's your relationship to deprivation? Take a few moments to focus on everything you don't have. Experiment with telling yourself that you *should* have it. Let yourself feel entitled. How does your view of yourself change when you see yourself as fundamentally deprived?

Further Reading: Classic Books about Hanging on and Letting Go

- Viktor E. Frankl, *Man's Search for Meaning*, Beacon, 2006.
- Elisabeth Kübler-Ross, MD, *On Death and Dying*, Scribner Classics, 1997.

19

Read the Instructions

RTFM. If you don't know what it means, you're going to have to look it up, because I don't want to get all explicit here. But it's one of my favorite internet acronyms, so neatly encapsulating the simple truth that, for the most part, we already have the information we need to make the things in our lives function properly. Take a few minutes to expand your awareness of your relationships to the objects around you by studying the instruction manual for one of your household appliances.

What You'll Need
• A common household appliance and its manual

How to Do It
1. **Choose a manual.** I know that somewhere in your house you have a drawer full of them. A random selection from my own drawer reveals instructions on how to work our programmable thermostat, our wireless

phone, our kitchen disposal unit, and our vacuum cleaner. Make sure to pick a manual for an object that you still own. And for best results, consider choosing one for an appliance that you don't understand particularly well.

2. **Study the appliance.** Before you learn about the appliance properly, do the thing that we all instinctively do: try to figure it out without the benefit of instructions. Start by staring at it blankly. Then push some of its buttons randomly, just to see what happens.

3. **Consider your relationship to the appliance.** This is important. Our relationships with the physical objects in our lives are profoundly shaped by our expectations of those objects. If you contemplate the appliance and let your mind go a little loose around the edges, all sorts of fascinating things will start happening. For instance, while staring at my thermostat, I find that my first thought is that I just want it to *work*. I don't want to have to understand *how* it works. My next thought is that I want it to work *perfectly*, without my intervention and without maintenance. If I let myself continue on this path, I'm certain that I could make my way to a projective portrait of my own deepest needs. Follow your own threads, wherever (and as far as) they lead.

4. **Read the manual.** And I mean *really* read it. From beginning to end. Look at the table of contents to see

how it's organized. Study the safety warnings, the installation instructions, and maintenance requirements. Immerse yourself fully in the workings of the appliance. Find out everything that it is capable of doing and where its limits lie. Finally, explore the troubleshooting guide and study the details of the product's warranty and registration procedures.

5. **Imagine the appliance as a friend.** Perhaps that sounds a little strange. But consider what you have just done in this exercise. It's the equivalent of listening really well to another person and to making a sincere effort to understand someone *on his or her own terms*. You have allowed your appliance to speak to you in its native tongue. Now place what you have learned up against the fantasies and projections you identified in step 3. What do you need from the appliance? What is it able to give you? See if you can imagine a more reality-based relationship with your appliance.

Material Culture

That's the term anthropologists use for the concrete objects that populate our daily lives. And although we don't usually think of it this way, those objects have lives of their own—the lives that we imbue them with through our unconscious projections. Whether we acknowledge it or not, we commonly treat inanimate objects as if they

were living beings. Consider the guy who kicks his car when it won't start. Or the person who lovingly tucks his or her iPod into its cradle at night. We might tell ourselves that our feelings are actually directed toward the *company* responsible for the object (which makes the object seem a little more personal). We hate Chevy, we love Apple, or whatever. But really, there remains an animist spirit deep down inside all of us that sees the entire physical universe as if it were made up of living things. In this way, our relationships with objects really are a mirror of our relationships with ourselves.

Variations: Instruct Yourself

Read the manual for a product you don't own. Or, even better, for a product you don't *understand*. (These manuals are easy to find online.) Pick an appliance category that seems the most mysterious to you. (Personally, I'm drawn to Panasonic's Indoor Pan/Tilt Head. I have no idea what it is, even when I stare at the manual.) Challenge your mind by trying to comprehend the internal logic of the instructions for an object you don't understand.

Open it up. Do so at your own risk, but do it with gusto. Find the part of some manual that gives you the stern warning that "no user-serviceable parts" are inside the appliance. You've been treating the appliance like a

black box that can only be understood from the outside. That's what they *want* you to believe. So open it up, void the warranty, and liberate yourself from the tyranny of artificial corporate boundaries. Think of it as brain surgery. Once you've got it open, you have a world of choices to make. You can disassemble the whole thing if you like (and if you're willing to sacrifice the appliance). Or you can just stare in wonder at the mystery of the mechanics contained within as you experience the freedom of escorting yourself into the forbidden territory of the interior lives of appliances.

Write a manual for yourself. This is self-explanatory and highly entertaining, but not easy. Take a manual for the appliance that you feel most resembles you. (Are you more like a phone or a smoke alarm? Are you a vacuum cleaner or a thermostat?) Following the structure of the manual you have chosen, rewrite the manual substituting yourself for the appliance.

Write a manual for someone else. This is much harder, of course, because you don't *really* have access to the information you need. You are forced to rely a great deal on conjecture and intuition. Choose an appliance that resembles someone you feel you know well; then rewrite the manual substituting their personality for the appliance. If you're really daring, show it to them after you've done it.

Further Reading: Books on the Workings and History of Appliances and Devices

- Gardner D. Hiscox, *1800 Mechanical Movements: Devices and Appliances*, Dover Publications, 2007.
- Edward Spencer Keene, *Mechanics of the Household: A Course of Study Devoted to Domestic Machinery and Household Mechanical Appliances (1918)*, Kessinger Publishing, 2008.
- Daniel Miller, ed., *Material Cultures: Why Some Things Matter*, University of Chicago Press, 1998.
- Sherry Turkle, ed., *The Inner History of Devices*, MIT Press, 2008.

20

Give Thanks

But not the way you usually do. Practice being thankful to a person in your past whom you found utterly irritating and unpleasant. That person is a messenger delivering important news to you about yourself. You just have to figure out how to decipher the message.

What You'll Need
- Your memory

How to Do It
1. **Identify the irritant.** Focus on a single person and limit your selection to someone who is no longer in your life. Go back as far as you'd like. A few candidates will probably come to mind right away. It might be an elementary school classmate who teased you mercilessly or a college roommate with poor hygiene and no social skills. Just make sure that the very thought of that person makes you shiver with discomfort.

2. **Magnify the irritant.** Now bring that person more fully into your mind. First picture him or her in as much visual detail as you can. Remember the sound of his or her voice and scent. Then bring to mind the scene or incident involving that person that most characterizes the irritating qualities. If you can't remember specific details, don't worry about it; just make up a narrative based on the essential qualities of that person. What you invent will be true enough.

3. **Watch the scene from the perspective of a neutral observer.** Now take that same scene and replay it, but this time watch it as if it were a movie. Put yourself in the back row of an empty theater and watch yourself interacting with the irritating person from your past. To do this, you'll need to re-create the image of yourself at the time. Take a moment to imagine your past self as fully and honestly as you can. Don't leave out your own quirks and shortcomings.

4. **Create an alternate explanation.** Assume the role of an unrelentingly optimistic anthropologist from outer space whose job is to create an explanation for what is shown on the screen. Find a way to describe the irritating behavior as a generous gift. You're free to get very creative and even fantastical in your explanation. But don't use masochism, deprivation, or any negative feelings in this redefinition. The alternate

explanation can't be that you secretly enjoyed being teased or that you actually liked the smell of body odor. It must be genuinely positive.

5. **Give thanks.** A proper thank-you acknowledges the gift that was received and describes how that gift is meaningful to the recipient. Formulate that sentence; then say it out loud.

Adventures in Reframing

My first exposure to this sort of exercise came in graduate school, when a professor with a Jungian bent asked us to close our eyes and imagine the person who had aggravated us more than anyone else we could think of. An old co-worker immediately sprang to my mind: her icky intrusiveness, her passive-aggressive manner. Even her name made me cringe.

After we had summoned this irritating person back into our minds, the professor said a truly horrible thing.

"The reason this person bothers you so much," she said, "is because he or she embodies the unexpressed side of your *own* personality. This person is the embodiment of your shadow self."

She took it a step further and instructed us to come to the next class dressed and behaving as that person. I recoiled at the whole idea. But I had to participate, and I did my best to let myself be aware that the qualities I most

identified as being "not me" were in fact parts of me that I didn't want to acknowledge. The truth in this was revealed in the sense of pleasure that crept in as I allowed myself to act out the irritating person's behavior. There *was* a part of me that wanted to be just this annoying, in just this way. And expressing it wasn't nearly as bad as I'd feared.

Variations: Gratitude, Forgiveness, and Loving-Kindness

Find gratitude for mistakes. This exercise focuses on individual *people*. But it can also work quite nicely with a focus on *actions* from our past. Try doing the same exercise with a focus on a specific mistake that you have made in the past, something that really makes you wince when you remember it. Reframe that incident in a way that genuinely makes it positive. Our mistakes are part of what makes us who we are. See if you can celebrate them.

Add forgiveness. Forgiveness is a rich and difficult subject. It's typically the domain of religion, but it certainly doesn't reside there only. The very definition of forgiveness is a matter of debate, so for our purposes here you can define it any way that makes sense to you. Using the people and actions that you have been thinking about during this exercise, experiment with adding the phrase, "I forgive you." And if you really want to push the limits, try adding this: "I also forgive myself."

Adopt a loving-kindness meditation. Also known as metta meditation, this Buddhist practice is designed to help bring a quality of equanimity to our experience of love. That's to say, it's meant to help us feel and express love not only toward those people in our lives whom we find inherently loveable, but also to all living beings. Although there are many variations, the basic formula is simple and can be done without any formal training in meditation. You start by focusing on yourself while reciting some version of these phrases:

> May I be peaceful and happy.
> May I be healthy.
> May I be safe and protected.
> May I have ease of well-being.

Then move your focus outward, reciting the same wishes first for someone you love as unconditionally as possible, someone you feel neutral about, someone who causes you difficulty, and then out to the world as a whole.

Further Reading: Books on the Shadow, Forgiveness, and Loving-Kindness

- Robert Bly, *A Little Book on the Human Shadow*, Harper & Row, 1988.
- Richard Holloway, *On Forgiveness: How Can We Forgive the Unforgivable?* Canongate, 2002.

- Robert A. Johnson, *Owning Your Own Shadow: Understanding the Dark Side of the Psyche*, HarperCollins, 1991.
- Nawang Khechog, *Awakening Kindness: Finding Joy Through Compassion for Others*, Atria Books/Beyond Words, 2010.
- Sharon Salzberg, *Lovingkindness: The Revolutionary Art of Happiness*, Shambhala, 1995.
- Desmond Mpilo Tutu, *No Future Without Forgiveness*, Doubleday, 1999.

Hide

Imagine there's a search party after you. Hide anywhere you want—even in plain sight—but imagine that wherever you are, it is impossible for anyone to find you. You can be pursued endlessly and be absolutely safe. Feel the powerful energy that resides in the space between absolute danger and absolute safety.

What You'll Need
- Your imagination

How to Do It
1. **Get scared.** Start by generating a nonspecific sense of fear. Do this by imitating the physiological correlates of fear in your body. Tighten your stomach while taking quick and shallow breaths. Clench other muscle groups as well. Look from side to side rapidly. Notice as you do all this how your physical state actually creates an emotional state within you, even when it's done

107

artificially. (Note: A little of this can go a long way. If you are a person who is highly prone to anxiety or panic attacks, consider skipping this step or only doing it very briefly.)

2. **Create the search party.** Feel free to make them really bad guys. Pretend that you're Julie Andrews as Maria, sneaking the von Trapp children out of Nazi Austria at the end of *The Sound of Music*. Or that you're Harrison Ford in *The Fugitive*. If you want to intensify the exercise, consider choosing someone from whom you are actually hiding in real life—an ex-lover or someone you owe money. Whomever you pick, imagine them in vivid visual detail.

3. **Set the scene.** Why are they after you? Create a scenario in which they are desperate to get you. If you are using real people, feel free to exaggerate the situation beyond the confines of reality. Make it into a life-or-death issue.

4. **Hide!** Look around. They're hot on your trail and you've got to find someplace to hide—and quick! There's probably nowhere that's actually decent to hide, and you're going to feel like the fat character in a cartoon who tries to hide behind a skinny telephone pole. That's just fine. Just make sure that you actually physically get fully into a hiding position.

5. **Relax and let them look.** Because they're never going to find you. Quite by accident, you have stum-

bled onto a hiding place so unbelievably perfect that they can stand right in front of you, looking directly into your eyes, and still not see you. You can make all the noise you want, and they won't hear you. Try to hold it all in your mind at once—the severity of the threat with a simultaneous sense of deep safety. Can you feel the fear and the comfort at the same time, or is it just too much to hold? Either way, it's fine. Enjoy the sense of triumph and try to carry it with you as you move through the rest of your day.

Hidden in Plain Sight

As part of my postgraduate psychotherapy training in attachment, I spent a great deal of time watching videotapes of parents interacting with their children. The point was to be able to identify communication and behavior patterns that signaled problems in these relationships, and to figure out ways to help these parents provide their children with a more secure base from which they could explore the world.

The most important thing I learned from watching all these interactions was that nearly everything I needed to know to help a parent was right there in front of my eyes. It was there in that split second in which a flash of contempt crossed a mother's face as she looked at her child. It was there in the child's helpless expression when her

father turned his back on her. I noticed it as it happened, but for some reason I discounted its importance. We all did, until the trainer froze the tape and we were forced to see what our minds didn't want to accept. It was, as my teachers had put it, hidden in plain sight. We just needed to learn to see it.

We've all got a version of this blind spot. It's the reason why sociopaths can find it so easy to hide their true identity. If they make themselves look like model citizens, they know that no one will want to believe that they are pedophiles or serial killers. They use our blind spots to their own advantage. We might sense that there's something "off" about the guy, but we're just too polite to freeze the tape at the right moment so that we can discover the truth.

While that's a grim (but instructive) example, this dynamic is operating in all our ordinary relationships. Is it possible to see the world without the blinders that keep you from seeing others clearly? Try taking off the blinders and opening your eyes.

Variations: Hide and Seek

Hide an object. Try to figure out how to hide an unusual object in plain sight. Your impulse might be to focus on the object, but try instead to think about how people scan their physical environment. What do they notice? What do they ignore?

Hide from people who aren't looking for you. My children *love* this game. They often play it when we're walking along a lightly trafficked street. They go along, having an ordinary conversation, and then whenever a car approaches, they dive for cover. It's endlessly satisfying, and it works nicely on a busy city street as well. Just stand still in an unobtrusive spot and watch how many people don't see you at all.

Find someone else. If you're not careful, this can edge up on stalking, so try to use good judgment if you do it. Standing still in a crowded public place (a mall, say, or a concert, or a busy street), pick out one person and track them with your eyes for a few moments. Don't be creepy about it; just notice them. How much can you actually see about a person simply from observing their outward behavior? (Hint: it's more than you think you can.)

What's blocking your vision? "We don't see things as they are; we see them as we are." The quote is attributed to both Anaïs Nin and the Talmud, but the truth behind it remains: our perceptions are not a literal recording of reality, but rather an *interpretation* of reality that derives from our experience and our beliefs, our culture, and even our mood. Try to get a glimpse of your own interpretive bias by catching yourself in an unfounded snap judgment about another person (that *lazy* homeless person; that *selfish* driver who just cut

you off) and forcing yourself to see the person in a different way.

Further Reading: Books on Hiding and the Hidden

- Michael Connor, *How to Hide Anything*, Paladin Press, 1984.
- Robert D. Hare, PhD, *Without Conscience: The Disturbing World of the Psychopaths Among Us*, Guilford Press, 1999.
- Jack Luger, *Big Book of Secret Hiding Places*, Breakout Productions, 1999.
- J. J. Luna, *How to Be Invisible: The Essential Guide to Protecting Your Personal Privacy, Your Assets, and Your Life*, Thomas Dunne Books, 2004.
- Martha Stout, PhD, *The Sociopath Next Door: The Ruthless Versus the Rest of Us*, Broadway Books, 2005.

22

Get Lost

The previous exercise, Hide, was a meditation on security. Here, a slight shift in perspective transforms that exercise into a meditation on disorientation. Rather than imagining that you cannot be found, imagine that you don't know where you are.

What You'll Need
- A familiar place

How to Do It
1. **Choose a place.** It could be a room in your house, a public park, a safe spot in the woods, or anyplace else where you feel safe and comfortable when by yourself. The point is to give youself a secure location from which to explore insecurity.
2. **Refamiliarize yourself with the place.** Take a moment to let yourself feel how well you know the space you have chosen. Look around you and notice

the familiar landmarks. Think of objects as landmarks, even if you are inside a room. They are the physical entities that help you navigate this particular space.

3. **Lose yourself.** There are several approaches to "losing" yourself in a familiar place. The first involves a cognitive trick: try to force yourself to see the place as if you've never seen it before. The second is to try to disregard the physical environment and create a state of mind-blindness, in which you can't really even take in the objects around you. Choose the method that feels right for you (or feel free to invent one of your own). However you do it, try to create the sort of state of mind that you experience when you wake up abruptly after having nodded off in an unfamiliar place.

4. **Panic.** Just a little. Because this jolt of fear is what gives being lost its power. Tell yourself that you will *never* find your way home from this place. Let yourself imagine for just a moment that your life has suddenly taken a dramatic turn. There's no going back. Try to remain in this fearful state for a few moments without doing anything about it. Notice as much about it as you possibly can.

5. **Stumble back into reality.** When you're ready, find your way back to a state of mind in which you know where you are. As you do this, try not to let yourself rely on any particular skill or capacity. In other words,

don't figure it out. Rather, let it be random and accidental, as if you simply woke up and found yourself back in a familiar place without knowing how you got there. See how fully you can experience the physical and emotional transition from fear to security.

The Value of Being Lost

Everyone is different in his or her capacity to tolerate disorientation.

Personally, I have a hard time *actually* getting physically lost. I grew up in the West and I learned almost intuitively to orient myself geographically. I can wander endlessly in the mountains of Montana where I live, and my mind will unconsciously track drainages and ridgelines. I always know exactly how to get myself back to where I started. I may not be able to tell you (at least on a cloudy day) what actual direction I'm headed in. I'm not a human GPS. But I have a strong internal sense of how to get around.

I think that's why part of me really enjoys the sensation of losing my way, whether it's geographically, emotionally, or psychologically. It's not that I'm not fearful and anxious when this happens. I certainly am. But there's an energizing excitement that accompanies the fear. There's a puzzle to be solved.

Of course, although we don't allow ourselves to be conscious of it most of the time, being lost is an essential

part of being human. We create an illusion of orientation by sticking close to our own familiar community and culture, surrounding ourselves with the people and objects that orient us to our environment. But as soon as we move beyond our comfort zone—by traveling to a foreign country, say, or simply by contemplating the vastness of the universe—our heads start to spin. It's that head-spinning disorientation that makes being lost so valuable. Being lost drives us to search for meaning and connection. And that search opens us to creative possibilities that aren't accessible when we have the luxury and comfort of knowing exactly where we stand.

Variations: Orientation and Disorientation

Lose an object. Yes, I know—you do it all the time anyway. But try doing it on purpose. Take an object that you regularly lose track of (a key ring is always a good choice here, or a wallet) and put it somewhere in plain sight. Then look everywhere else for it, trying to feel some of the urgency you feel when you think you've lost something important. What is it like to know that you have the information you need, but not allow yourself access to that information?

Spin in place. There's no simpler way to experience temporary disorientation than simply spinning in place until you're too dizzy to walk straight. Try doing it by setting a simple geographical goal ahead of time (the front door, say). As you spin in place, remember what it felt like when you first discovered this sensation as a child, the realization that you have the power to transform your own internal sensations. As you come out of the spin, move as quickly as you can toward your geographical goal. How deeply can you experience this temporary loss of your ability to navigate the world?

Actually get lost. This is an advanced exercise, so it's important that you set up a few safety mechanisms before you start. Pick a spot in an unfamiliar outdoor place (a park you've never been to before, perhaps) where you can clearly identify an escape route. Perhaps there is a visible orienting landmark (a mountain or a tall building) that you can ignore until you need it. Put yourself in the middle of your identified space; then occupy your mind with a deeply absorbing mental question. As you do this, begin to walk in spiraling circles outward from the center. Continue moving at off-angles, trying not to look up at or take in your surroundings in any way. When it feels like you've gone far enough, stop walking and close your eyes. You might even spin around once or twice. Then open your eyes and see if you have truly gotten yourself lost. If so, good for you! Take a moment to notice the twinge of fear. Then go ahead and find your way back.

Further Reading: Getting Lost and Finding Your Way

- Steven Boga, *Orienteering*, Stackpole Books, 1997.
- Tim Cresswell, *Place: A Short Introduction*, Blackwell Publishing, 2004.
- Harold Gatty, *Finding Your Way Without Map or Compass*, Dover Publications, 1999.
- Rebecca Solnit, *A Field Guide to Getting Lost*, Viking, 2005.

23

Make a List

A good list can completely shift your perspective on any goal or problem. In this exercise we'll take list making to the extreme.

What You'll Need
- Paper and pen
- An impossibly optimistic long-term goal

How to Do It
1. **Pick a goal.** Keep it positive and make it long-term and seemingly impossible to achieve. For instance, *I will reduce my carbon emissions to zero*. Or, *I will never fight with my spouse again*.
2. **Feel just how impossible it is.** Start by taking a minute to try to talk yourself out of even trying to achieve it. Tell yourself that it's impossible and that it could never happen. Ask yourself, "What's the point?" Then sigh and say to yourself, "So-and-so says I have to."

3. **Make a broad outline.** Feel free to stay sulky as you start this step. Ask yourself, "If it were somehow possible that I could never fight with my spouse again, what would it take?" Start with the broadest strokes and make a short list: *we'd have to be able to communicate better; we'd have to learn to anticipate fights before they happened; we'd have to figure out how to respectfully disagree.*

4. **Subdivide.** Pick one item from the list you just made—whatever feels like a reasonable starting point—and break it down further. Make a list of three or four things you'd have to do to achieve it. Then repeat this process, taking one item from *that* list and breaking it down further. Continue repeating these steps until you have arrived at something that feels more or less irreducible. In the end, the path of your thinking might look something like this: *In order to anticipate fights before they happen, I need to be more aware of what triggers me into anger. In order to that, I need to become more mindful of the experience of anger in my daily life. To do that, I need to keep a record of every time I start to feel anger during a typical day. To do that, I'd need to have a pad that I could keep in my pocket. There's a pad like that in my desk. To get it, I'd need to get up out of my chair.*

5. **Take the first step.** This is all you need to do right now: get up out of your chair. Do it, and do it mindfully. After you're done with the exercise, feel free to go back to your list and move on to the other steps you've

identified. But for *this* moment, simply focus on the act of getting up out of your chair, staying mindful of the fact that in doing so you are moving toward a future in which you will never again fight with your spouse.

My Mother's Formula

"Make a list!"

That's what I heard from my mother every time I would complain to her about a task or a problem that was overwhelming me. She always said it cheerfully. It seemed to genuinely make her happy to think of how manageable the world started to seem when you broke things down into a list. But honestly, it drove me completely crazy, partly because what I wanted from her was simple commiseration. I wanted her to agree with me that my life was miserable and that there was no possible solution to my problems. But more than that, what bothered me was that she was *right*. Breaking down a problem into its component parts, transforming something *external* (the science fair project I had to get done) into something *internal* (the list of tasks that *I* had created) almost always helped me. Looking back on it, most interesting to me was the fact that it worked even when I was actively refusing to believe that it could. We are not always in as much control of our state of mind as we would like to believe.

Variations: Conceptual Subdivision

Attend Measurement 101. Measurement (as you might remember a long-ago elementary school teacher telling you) is not an absolute concept. The degree of accuracy of any measurement is determined by the size of the unit of measurement being used. And because there is no limit to how small a unit of measurement can be, there is no such thing as absolute accuracy in measurement. This exercise works by applying smaller and smaller "units of measurement" to a list. Spend a few minutes contemplating the implications of measurement on your list. How could you subdivide your list even further? At what point does the precision of the unit of measurement begin to be counterproductive? Why does this happen?

Explore concordance. A concordance is simply a list of all the words used in a particular book (or set of books) arranged alphabetically and/or by frequency. There are dozens of concordances of the Bible. But they exist for other authors and texts as well. What is the most frequently used seven-letter word in Shakespeare? There's a book out there that will tell you that. It's a fascinating way to generate new insights into a familiar text. You can also create concordances from your own life. Try it, using the last ten emails you sent to your best friend. You might be surprised by what your rearranged words reveal.

Confound yourself with fractals. Fractals are shapes that, when subdivided, are (at least roughly) smaller versions of the thing they came off of. Think of how a broccoli floret has the same shape and form as an entire head of broccoli. Fractals confound list making by essentially eliminating the variation that makes lists meaningful. Try it with lists. Can you imagine a task that is endlessly recursive—a task where a list of the subtasks is essentially a repetition of the larger task?

Think globally, act locally. Yes, I'm not ashamed to admit it: this exercise is a variation on a bumper sticker. Try doing the exercise using a global goal in step 1. Try saying this goal: *I will reverse global warming.* Or, *I will create world peace.* Your list will then become a way of identifying a specific local step that you could take in order to achieve the global goal.

Further Reading: Books on Lists, Categories, and Measurement

- Sasha Cagen, *To-Do List: From Buying Milk to Finding a Soul Mate, What Our Lists Reveal About Us*, Fireside/ Simon & Schuster, 2007.
- Atul Gawande, *The Checklist Manifesto: How to Get Things Right*, Metropolitan Books, 2009.
- Christopher Joseph, ed., *A Measure of Everything: An Illustrated Guide to the Science of Measurement*, Firefly, 2005.

- Benoit B. Mandelbrot, *The Fractal Geometry of Nature*, W. H. Freeman, 1983.
- Caroline Adams Miller, MAPP, and Dr. Michael B. Frisch, *Creating Your Best Life: The Ultimate Life List Guide*, Sterling, 2009.
- Andrew Robinson, *The Story of Measurement*, Thames & Hudson, 2007.

24

Pace

You know those scenes from 1940s screwball movies in which the harried executive is pacing back and forth in a too-small office, hands behind his back, a cigar clenched between his teeth? It's a beautifully absurd expression of a certain sort of moment in our universal human experience, when an intense need meets an intractable barrier. Take a few minutes to enact this scene and allow yourself to experience the pent-up energy concealed within the present moment.

What You'll Need
- A small room
- Something to hold between your teeth

How to Do It
1. **Pick a room and a fake cigar.** You can do this exercise in any space—even a very large room—simply by mentally defining a small space in which to pace. But

the effect is going to be best if you are in fact literally walled in. (The perfect room, if you happen to have access to it, would probably be your childhood bedroom.) It's also nice to have an open door you can pace in front of so that you can imagine the comic effect you have on someone standing outside. Decide exactly how far you will go in each direction before you turn. Finally, pick something you can chew on, ideally something soft that you can really sink your teeth into.

2. **Choose an attitude.** Pacing can be an expression of many different sorts of pent-up desires. Perhaps it's the frustration of a narcissistic executive who can't get his employees to do what he wants. Or the sadistic anticipation of an evil villain. But it can also be the good-hearted anxiety of a hero who is trying to figure out how to rescue someone in trouble. The common element is frustration and a temporary inability to achieve one's goals. Think of something in your life that you can't have right now. Then blow it up into comic-book proportions. If what you want is a new car, imagine that it is something you *could* have except for that one blockhead (here you can insert a blockhead of your choice, fictional or real) who is keeping you from getting it.

3. **Assume the position.** The pose is extremely important for this exercise. All the emotion of angry desire

and frustration is contained within it. Put the cigar-like object between your teeth and bite down hard. This will automatically place your face in a growling expression. Put your arms behind your back, palms facing backwards, gripping one wrist with the other hand. Then, keeping your legs straight, bend at the hips. Think of the Penguin in the old *Batman* show. This should feel a little strange. Hold the position for a few moments. Settle into it.

4. **Growl. Then start to move forward.** Starting from one side of the too-small space, start walking. Move slowly at first, maintaining as best you can the physical position you assumed in step 3. Keep your head down and try to walk on the back of your heels. Then, when you reach the boundary line, pause for a moment, snap your head up, and swivel 180 degrees. Repeat this movement in the opposite direction. Holding in mind the frustrated desire you identified in step 2, keep repeating this motion, gradually increasing your pace. As you speed up, the subtleties of the head snap and swivel will wash away. That's fine, but do try to maintain the overall posture. Continue until you're moving just a little faster than feels comfortable. Once you're in a rhythm, really let yourself feel the pent-up desire for the thing you can't have. Feel it as a matter of life or death.

5. Stop! Do this step quickly, without thinking about it. Throw your hands up in the air and shout, "I've got it!" Now, of course you don't actually "have it" at all, but let yourself behave as if the solution has just come to you. Without letting yourself think about the problem itself, feel what it's like to have a solution. Spit out whatever you've got in your mouth, relax your face and the rest of your body, and let the energy expand and spread through you.

Going Nowhere Fast

When we face a problem that feels insoluble, the dread that arises can be intense. We can quickly move to catastrophic thinking: "I will never be able to move past this point for the rest of my life." It's not true, of course. Like an old-fashioned serial that ends with the hero in a seemingly impossible situation, unexpected openings will appear soon enough. But anxiety (just like depression) can constrict our vision and temporarily blind us to different ways of approaching a problem. Anxiety blocks creativity and inhibits flexibility in our thinking. We become like a revving engine that we can't get into gear or, even worse, like a car with the brake and gas pedals pushed down at the same time.

Most people, when you tell them you're feeling this way, will tell you to slow down and relax. This exercise obviously takes a different approach. That's because sometimes the way through a problem is actually *through* it. It may sound strange to say, but paralysis has its benefits. Even when it feels like you're in the tightest of situations, there's always a little bit of room for movement. It may be nothing more than rocking back and forth or tapping your fingers. But when you embrace your capacity for motion, when you begin to intensify that motion, you allow your mind to start seeing things in new and unexpected ways.

Variations: Pick Up the Pace

Rock. As I mentioned, the act of pacing is simply a comic and dramatic version of a state of mind in which we can't see a way forward. Try doing a minimalist version of this exercise in which you sit down, hunch over in a semifetal position, and simply rock. You can do this using the attitude you chose in step 2, or you can rock with no focus at all.

Hit the wall. Try introducing a variation based on the popular children's activity of simply moving forward until you run into a barrier, and then reversing your direction until you hit the barrier on the other side of the room. It's a sort of enforced pacing, which really heightens the sense of inflexible external limitations.

Introduce indecision. Sometimes pacing is not so much about finding a solution to a problem as it is about

choosing between two options. Try pacing with a yes-or-no decision in mind. Start with a decision that's a bit ridiculous (chocolate or vanilla, say), but act it as if everything depends on it. Resolve the episode in any way you choose, or don't bother to resolve it at all.

Further Reading: Books on Feeling Stuck and Going Nowhere

- Ajahn Brahm, *Who Ordered This Truckload of Dung?: Inspiring Stories for Welcoming Life's Difficulties*, Wisdom Publications, 2005.
- Ayya Khema, *Being Nobody, Going Nowhere: Meditations on the Buddhist Path*, Wisdom Publications, 2001.
- Anneli Rufus, *Stuck: Why We Can't (or Won't) Move On*, Jeremy P. Tarcher/Penguin, 2008.

25

Moan

Moaning is misunderstood. It's commonly used as a synonym for complaining. But when babies do it, we think it's sweet. And when monks do it, we call it chanting. And really, moaning is just sound waves—vibrations. The world is made up of vibrations. And you are part of the world. Use the natural capacity of your body to reclaim your natural place in the vibratory world.

What You'll Need
- Your vocal chords (to provide the sound)
- Your body (the resonating chamber)
- A small, contained space, like a bathroom or a shower

How to Do It
1. **Inhale.** Inhale deeply, until you feel your breath pushing against your stomach.
2. **Hold your breath.** Take a moment to feel the upward pressure in your throat.

3. **Moan.** Keeping your mouth closed with your lips pressed together gently (this magnifies the vibration), slowly push air through your throat while making a humming sound. Start with a simple humming moan, at whatever pitch naturally emerges. Let the air slowly escape until the moan dies off. The sound will break up a little at the conclusion of the moan. This is natural.

4. **Introduce tone and volume.** Repeating the process described above, experiment with how high and low you can make your moan go before the sound dies out. Next, play with volume. How softly can you moan while still making sound? What happens to the quality of the moan as you increase the volume? How much noise can you make before the moan becomes a bellow?

5. **Enjoy it.** Find the pitch and pace that feel most satisfying; then relax and feel the vibration. Turn your attention to the physical experience of sound. Tune in to each part of your body and let yourself fully experience the vibratory effects. When you're done, take a few deep breaths and enjoy the energy that now infuses your body. Let that energy carry you forward into whatever you have to do next.

An Empty Vessel

Moaning can mean *anything*. Its very shapelessness gives it an incredible expressive power. Depending on the context, we can recognize the same formless noise as an expression of intense pain, deep grief, frustration, anger, or sexual ecstasy. And without context it can be very hard to figure out the meaning of a moan. At the core, it is simply sound—vibration. And the vibrations created through moaning create a physical effect on your body, a sort of gentle touch. In this way, a moan can actually be a way of holding ourselves.

I discovered this years ago when, after a major surgery, I awoke too soon in the recovery room. Truly, it was the stuff of horror movies: the anesthesia was still paralyzing my body, but it was no longer blocking the intense post-operative pain. I could move my eyes enough to see other anesthetized patients on gurneys around me and a nurse somewhere in the distance. I tried to speak, but I couldn't make my mouth move. I knew that I wasn't in any danger, but I still had to figure out some way to endure the pain. But the *only* thing I could manage to do was moan. So that's what I did. And as I did, I realized that it was actually helping me with the pain. When I found the right pitch, the vibration was soothing. The sound of the moaning eventually brought the nurse over to attend to me. Since that time I've never forgotten how powerfully healing the sound of my own voice can be. Try it the next time you're in pain. Focus on the pain, and then find a pitch to moan at that soothes the hurt. It really works!

Variations: More Experiments with Moaning

Open your mouth. This reduces the intensity of the sensation inside your body while creating interesting new attitudes.

Do it to music. Think of music as modulated moaning. Put on the blues, Gregorian chants, or some Tuvan throat singing (I've provided a few musical suggestions in the next section) and start moaning along.

Groan. It's not the same thing, you know. Groaning has a more specific emotional tone, and is composed of a slightly different set of physical maneuvers. Try it, and see if you can identify the difference.

Add feelings! You might find that moaning naturally allows feelings—both positive and negative—to rise to the surface. You can also experiment with feelings by invoking them intentionally. Try moaning while thinking about complaints. Moan while feeling sorry for yourself. Moan with delight. It's a great way to let yourself safely experience the full intensity of these natural feelings.

Further Listening: Selected Music to Moan With

- Benedictine Monks of Santo Domingo de Silos, *Chant*, Angel (CDC 555138), 1994.
- Blind Lemon Jefferson, *Black Snake Moan*, Gramercy Records, 2004.

- Howlin' Wolf, *Moanin' in the Moonlight*, Chess Records (1434), 1959.
- Huun-Huur-Tu, *Spirits from Tuva*, Paras Recordings (PRC 1134), 2003.
- Sara Martin, *The Famous Moanin' Mama: 1922–1927*, Challenge Records (CHL RTR79028), 2001.

26

Pose a Threat

Select a threat to world peace and enact it with a melodramatic pose. Imagine yourself as Kim Jong Il, your finger hovering over a bright-red nuclear launch button. Hold the pose and let yourself feel the destructive impulse. Then find the smallest change that you can make in the pose that will shift its energy from threat to safety.

What You'll Need
- A fantasy of destruction

How to Do It
1. **Choose your evil villain.** The least emotionally charged method is to keep things in the realm of comic book fantasy, using a character like *The Simpsons'* Mr. Burns. You can also invent a generic villain, or you can really challenge yourself by using actual historical bad guys like Hitler and Stalin or contemporary icons of evil like Osama bin Laden.

2. **Choose your pose.** Let your inner drama queen emerge. Imagine yourself as Norma Desmond *playing* Mr. Burns as you align your temporarily inflated ego with the fate of the planet. Choose a moment that is just on the edge of destruction. Maybe it's a finger on a button. But don't forget that sometimes destructive gestures hinge on mundane triggers. Maybe it's just your signature at the bottom of a legal document or a single code word uttered over a phone line. Whatever it is, find the physical pose that dramatically signifies the destruction you are about to unleash.

3. **Cackle.** Really. I mean it. Do your best mad scientist laugh. Feel your power. As you do this, feel free to rub your fingers together and say something like, "Now I shall rule the world!"

4. **Freeze.** This is the moment at the end of the old *Batman* television show (a great source of evil villains to model, by the way) when the voice-over narrator comes in and asks the ultimate question: "Is this really the *end* for the Caped Crusader?" Feel your power. Savor it.

5. **Shift.** If this were a television show, Batman would burst through the door right now, salvation arriving from the outside. But in this exercise, he's not coming. Instead, you need to split your character into two parts: the evil impulse and the rational observer. Letting the

evil impulse hover on the edge of destruction, bring in the rational observer and let it assess the situation. Ask it, "What is the simplest possible shift in this pose that would remove the danger?" The rational observer would say, "If only you would *relax your hand*, then no one would get hurt." Or, "If only you would *close your eyes*, all this destruction could be avoided." Or, "If only you would *relax your face* ..." Isolate a single gesture that will defuse the threat. Then make the shift. Feel the contrast between imminent destruction and security, in the world and in yourself.

Wouldn't My Time Be Better Spent Visualizing World Peace?

Well, you have a point there.

You could make a decent argument that *imagining* evil destruction only creates more destructive energy in the world. But you could also make a good argument that denying and suppressing aggressive urges only serves to intensify them, and that discharging them in nondestructive fantasies ultimately reduces the violent energy.

It's similar to the debates on violence in the media and video games. Do they make those who watch or use them more violent? The answer is necessarily complex in that it depends entirely on the character and development of the individual person. Someone who has been badly damaged in the past and who is trying to motivate himself or herself to go on a shooting spree could certainly use a violent video game to kindle those fantasies into action. But another type of person, the one that most of us are, might spend an hour playing *Grand Theft Auto* and come away from the experience a bit numb but otherwise just as compassionate and loving as when he or she started.

That's why, when parents ask me about the appropriateness of violent video games or movies for their child, I usually ask them to describe for me the quality of their relationship with that child. Does the child come to the parents for help in organizing his or her feelings, for instance? Is it the sort of relationship in which angry or aggressive feelings can be openly expressed and contained? Usually in the course of answering, parents find for themselves the answer to their own question.

In my view, acknowledging, exploring, and understanding aggressive and destructive impulses and feelings, in ourselves as well as in others, usually defuses rather than increases that energy. So for the sake of this exercise, I have gone ahead and made several assumptions about you. First, I assume that you are not preparing to go on a shooting spree. (Somehow, I just don't think this is the book you'd be reading if you were.) Second, I assume that you don't have the means of mass destruction at your fingertips. And finally, I assume that you are the sort of

person who actually *does* spend part of your time visualizing world peace.

Variations: Destruction and Salvation

Go ahead—visualize world peace. You know that you want to.

Or not. Maybe you'd rather get more in touch with your inner evil villain. That's fine, too. Try doing the exercise without the shift in step 5. Sign the paper. Pull the trigger. Push the button. Find out how you'd feel on the other side of that decision.

Make it personal. You can also do this exercise using actual people from your life in the place of evil villains. Think of someone who has hurt you in some way. (This can get into deep emotional territory pretty fast, so proceed with caution. Consider starting with someone who has hurt your feelings in a *small* way, rather than jumping straight to someone who has caused you deep trauma.) Re-create the scene in which you felt hurt, isolating the physical posture (real or imagined) of the person who hurt you. Then assume that posture and proceed with rest of the exercise. What is the shift that will reestablish safety?

Further Reading: World Domination Made Simple

- André de Guillaume, *How to Rule the World: A Handbook for the Aspiring Dictator*, Chicago Review Press, 2005.

- Niccolò Machiavelli, *The Prince*, CreateSpace, 2009.
- Rob Osborne, *1000 Steps to World Domination*, AiT/PlanetLar, 2004.
- Erwin S. Strauss, *How to Start Your Own Country*, Paladin Press, 1999.
- Neil Zawacki, *How to Be a Villain: Evil Laughs, Secret Lairs, Master Plans, and More!!!* Chronicle Books, 2003.

27

Hold Your Breath

Take a few moments to experience how your life goes on in the temporary absence of one its most essential activities. No need for suffocation. Just hold your breath, trusting your own reflexes to bring the exercise to a sudden and satisfying end as your body surrenders and gives itself the air it needs.

What You'll Need
- Your lungs
- Something you're mad about
- A stubborn attitude

How to Do It
1. **Do nothing.** Sit still for a moment. Don't try to pay attention to your breathing. Quiet your mind. Don't *do* anything.
2. **Tune in to the rhythm of your breath.** Now start to focus. Notice your breathing without trying to

change it in any way. (This is impossible, of course. Bringing our attention to anything changes it in some way. Still, try.)

3. **Think of something that makes you really, really mad.** It might be as large as the planet Earth's global warming or as small as a toilet seat left up. It doesn't matter what it is as long as it has a real charge, so that when you bring it to mind, it immediately makes your heart start beating faster. (The particular tone of the anger will vary depending on the person and the subject. Notice whether your impulse is to direct the anger outward and rage or whether it's to hold it in and fume.) Then, thinking about the thing or situation that makes you angry, formulate a threat: "I'm going to hold my breath until it changes."

4. **Hold your breath.** The basic action is quite simple: Inhale quickly and deeply, filling your chest with air. Then close your lips and pinch your nose closed. (To enhance the effect, you can try closing your eyes and scrunching up your face.) Once you've done this, you've got about thirty seconds to a minute to attend to the experience of not breathing. How you experience it will vary, depending on your personal anger style. If you are someone who rages, you'll run out of breath more quickly and will probably experience a more harsh return to breathing. If you tend to

internalize your anger, you'll probably have a little bit more time. Either one is fine. The point is simply to pay as close attention as you can to the experience of not breathing. What do you notice happening in your body? What's your heart rate like? Are there any muscular movements? Notice the quality of your thoughts. Are they panicky, determined, or detached? And notice especially how your experience evolves as your body becomes increasingly depleted of oxygen. Create an image in your head to go with this sensation. Is it like a candle going out? A movie screen fading to black?

5. **Return to life.** At the moment when the urge to breathe becomes irresistible, pause for one last second. This is important. Notice how even in the throes of a deep physical urge, you have control and can make a choice. Then as you let the air in, notice the way in which you do it. Do you take big, quick gulps of air? Or do you have a slower, more gradual reentry? For the next few minutes, keep noticing how your body recovers. As your breathing begins to even out again, bring back into your mind the thing or situation that makes you mad. Has it changed at all in quality? Or does it still evoke exactly the same response from you? Either way is fine. Just notice it as you go about the rest of your day.

The Three-Year-Old's Point of View

It's hard to believe that there was once a time when we believed that we could punish someone else by holding our own breath. From an adult perspective, it's comic and sort of sweet. But when a child threatens to hold his or her breath out of anger, that child is completely serious.

It's all about power, of course. Children, being inherently powerless, are at a loss when their lack of power meets up with an intense desire. The result is a chaotic effort on the child's part to reverse the roles. But how can a small child gain power over an adult? In trying to answer this question, children's minds are likely to seek out moments in which an adult's attention shifted entirely to them and to their needs: when they were very sick, injured, or in danger. They think, "Here's a way to harness that power: I'll put myself in danger; then you'll have to pay attention to me/give me what I want."

Is it a primitive form of civil disobedience? Or is it, as the saying goes, like drinking poison and waiting for the other person to die?

Variations: Power and Powerlessness

Deepen your awareness of your own powerlessness.
It's the first step in every twelve-step program: "We came to acknowledge that we were powerless over ..." Many people can't easily get past that first phrase. The idea of

powerlessness can be terrifying. If this is your experience, you might try disconnecting the idea of power from your personal needs and desires. Experiment with your own powerlessness by making a list of things you are powerless over but that you also have no desire to control. I am powerless over the direction of the wind. I am powerless over the pattern of cracks in the sidewalk. I am powerless over the color of the shirt my neighbor will wear today. Get absurd, get abstract, and feel the liberation.

Meditate on the unchangeable. How much energy do you expend wishing for changes that are completely outside your influence? How much magical thinking do you do trying to come up with ways in which the unchangeable problems in your life might somehow disappear? Make a list of genuinely bothersome things in your own life you have no true power over: traffic, advertising, fluorescent lighting in stores, whatever. Experiment with different attitudes you can take toward these things, ranging from exercises in stubborn protest to cognitive reframing to deep acceptance.

Study effective protest techniques. Finally, try reversing these exercises entirely. Imagine that you have within your grasp the ability to change everything around you. Harness and transform the impotent rage that this exercise magnified into a feeling of infinite possibility. Things *can* change. Start by studying the masters. Read the writings of Gandhi and Martin Luther King Jr. and think about what it is that can change for the better in the world, and what you can do to help make it happen.

Further Reading: Books on Breathing and Nonviolent Protest

- Blandine Calais-Germain, *Anatomy of Breathing*, Eastland Press, 2006.
- Louis Fischer, ed., *The Essential Gandhi: An Anthology of His Writings on His Life, Work, and Ideas*, Vintage Books, 2002.
- Gay Hendricks, PhD, *Conscious Breathing: Breathwork for Health, Stress Release, and Personal Mastery*, Bantam Books, 1995.
- Martin Luther King Jr. and James Melvin Washington, ed., *A Testament of Hope: The Essential Writings and Speeches of Martin Luther King, Jr.*, HarperCollins, 1991.
- Al Lee and Don Campbell, *Perfect Breathing: Transform Your Life One Breath at a Time*, Sterling, 2009.
- Dennis Lewis, *Free Your Breath, Free Your Life: How Conscious Breathing Can Relieve Stress, Increase Vitality, and Help You Live More Fully*, Shambhala, 2004.
- Yogi Ramacharaka, *Science of Breath*, Classic House, 2008.

28

Feel Your Foot

Divorce yourself from the rest of your body and inhabit your foot. Imagine yourself as a tiny homunculus operating your foot as if it were a piece of heavy machinery. Immerse yourself fully in the life that your foot is leading as it helps you move through the world, step-by-step.

What You'll Need
- Your feet
- Room to take a few steps

How to Do It
1. **Stare at your feet.** Start by simply looking at your feet. In a sitting position, take off your socks and shoes and look closely at this most distant part of your body. Pay careful attention to all the folds and angles of your anatomy. Notice the texture of your skin. What distinctions can you make among bones, muscles, and veins? Keep staring until your feet start to look a little bit alien.

2. **Get numb.** In order to find your way into the interior life of your foot, do a reverse body scan on the rest of your body. Start by focusing your awareness on the crown of your head. Feel your awareness as a sort of anesthesia that is making your scalp go temporarily numb. Move your attention across the muscles of your face, neck, and shoulders, out through each arm to your hands, down through your torso, and into your legs. White out your body until you reach your ankles. Then, letting the rest of your body stay numb, focus on your feet and make them come alive. Feel them intensely.

3. **Visualize the world inside your feet.** Start by picking one foot (either one is fine) and imagining its interior anatomy: muscles, cartilage, and bone. Then create a fantasy version of that anatomy. Think of the sequence in Woody Allen's *"Everything You Always Wanted to Know About Sex * But Were Afraid to Ask"* in which his body is inhabited and coordinated by little humans inside him. Wiggle your toes and imagine what the control center for such complex physical movement might look like.

4. **Move your mind into your foot.** Now imagine that you are the little person inside your foot making your toes wiggle. It might be helpful to visualize the flight deck of the Starship *Enterprise*. Make yourself Captain Kirk, sitting in your swivel chair, directing the action

and monitoring what's going on outside through the use of screens and monitors.

5. **Take a step.** Stand up and, as slowly as you can, take a single step. Notice what a dramatic movement this simple motion is from the perspective of the inside of your foot. Feel the levitating rise and the precipitous forward fall. Feel the shock of impact on the ground. Notice how the sensation of impact changes as the foot moves from the heel to the sole and on to the toes. Take a few more steps, letting yourself feel both the ways in which you are in control of the movement and the ways in which it is in control of you. Finally, sit down again and let sensation gradually seep back into the rest of your body. As you do this, allow the little person inside your foot to expand until you fill your entire body once again.

Horse and Rider

This exercise heightens our awareness of how much of our physical action and visceral experience occurs beneath the level of our conscious awareness or control. In fact, our mind's relationship to our body in many ways resembles Freud's description of the relationship between the ego and the id, which he compared to the relationship between a rider and a horse: "The horse supplies the locomotor energy, while the rider has the privilege of deciding on the goal and of guiding the powerful animal's movements. But only too often there arises between the ego and the id the not precisely ideal situation of the rider being obliged to guide the horse along the path by which it itself wants to go" (1990, 96). Who is really in charge, the rider or the horse? Where does the balance of power lie between our unconscious energy (or our simple forward momentum) and our conscious intention? To what degree are you able to intentionally manipulate this relationship?

Variations: Adventures in Body Scanning

Feel the earth through the soles of your feet. This is an extremely simple technique that can quickly restore your connection to your own body and to the planet. Simply take off your shoes and put the soles of your feet in contact with the ground, floor, or whatever surface you happen to be on. It doesn't matter whether you're inside a building, even if you're on an upper floor of a high-rise building. Whatever surface you feel beneath your feet is connected to the earth. Focus your awareness on the line of contact between your feet and the ground. Feel the deep solidity of the earth beneath you. Imagine the energy of your feet extending all the way down into the earth's core.

Do a *proper* body scan. It's an easy technique that can quickly shift both your state of mind and your awareness of your body. Just focus your attention on some part

of your body, feeling what's there and noticing everything you can about it. Then slowly shift your attention through the rest of your body. (If you're rushed for time, even a very quick scan can help you shift your energy.) It's amazing how gracefully, almost effortlessly, this technique can bring us back to an awareness of ourselves in the present moment.

Check out the rest of your body. It's simple and straightforward: you can vary this exercise to focus intensely on any part of your body. Become the little man who regulates your right eyelid. Or how about your tongue?

Further Reading: Books on Body Awareness

- Christine Caldwell, *Getting Our Bodies Back: Recovery, Healing, and Transformation through Body-Centered Psychotherapy*, Shambhala, 1996.
- Sigmund Freud, *New Introductory Lectures on Psychoanalysis: The Standard Edition*, W. W. Norton, 1990.
- Thomas Hanna, *Somatics: Reawakening the Mind's Control of Movement, Flexibility, and Health*, Da Capo Press, 1988.
- Ian Macnaughton, *Body, Breath, and Consciousness: A Somatics Anthology*, North Atlantic Books, 2004.
- Andrea Olsen, *Bodystories: A Guide to Experiential Anatomy*, University Press of New England, 1988.

29

Levitate

"**Y**ou can do anything you want to, if you just put your mind to it."

My mother told me this when I was a child ... over and over again. I wanted to believe her, but something just didn't seem quite right about it. *Anything?* So I would test her theory by trying to make myself levitate. Does the fact that I never succeeded disprove her claim? Or does it just mean that I never "put my mind to it" fully enough?

What You'll Need
- Faith
- Imagination
- Determination

How to Do It
1. **Look up.** Let's just start there. Wherever you are, look above you. Not just at what's visible, though. See if you can focus on the empty air *between* you and the ceiling,

tree limbs, clouds, or whatever happens to be the next physical object in your field of vision. Try to "see" the air. Imagine that empty space as a liquid. Imagine it's becoming thick enough to support you, like seawater or amniotic fluid.

2. **Choose a position.** How would you like to levitate? Sitting, standing, or lying down? It's entirely up to you.

3. **Believe.** If you're religious, perhaps this will come easily. If you're a skeptic, this will probably be the hardest step in the exercise. Close your eyes and tell yourself that levitation is possible. Don't try to prove it to yourself. Simply state it as the truth and try to force your mind to follow. There's a good chance you won't be able to get your mind to go along with you. That's okay. Just try to stay with it until you have experienced some fleeting sense of possibility.

4. **Visualize zero gravity.** Close your eyes and let images of zero gravity come to mind. Think of astronauts doing a space walk. Or Superman. Whatever comes to mind is fine.

5. **Levitate.** With your eyes closed, *feel* what it would be like for your body to rise gently up off of the ground. Not too far—just an inch or two. Focusing on whatever part of your body is in physical contact with the ground, imagine the sensation of that contact suddenly loosening, softening. Feel yourself floating on a

cushion of air. Resist the urge to open your eyes and find out if you're actually doing it. After a few moments, whatever levitational sensation you've managed to generate will begin to dissipate. Don't fight it. Imagine yourself floating gently back down to earth. Feel the solidity of the surface that is now supporting you. And when you're ready, open your eyes.

The Incredible Fluidity of Belief

Some people have a deep capacity for faith. But many of us, especially when it comes to spiritual matters, spend our lives floating back and forth between cynicism and blind faith. Which side we land on can vary from moment to moment, depending on what's at stake. We tell ourselves that our beliefs are rational, sensible, and true. But as anyone who's ever been in a cult will tell you, our minds are *capable* of believing anything. In fact, we're capable of knowing that something is not true and believing it anyway. And we're just as capable of disbelieving something we know to be true. Under the right circumstances, even those with the deepest religious convictions can talk themselves into doubt, and the most committed atheists can have moments in which they wonder if maybe God does in fact exist.

What does this mean?

It means that belief is a decision.

It means that our minds truly have a mind of their own.

Variations: Magic, Faith, and Cynicism

Learn to create illusions. Magic tricks are probably the closest any of us will ever come to witnessing levitation. Not long ago, it was almost impossible to learn the secrets behind magic tricks. These days, for better or for worse, it's easy to find a video online that will show you how to create the illusion that you're levitating. Why not learn? In addition to the simple power trip that comes with messing with people's perceptions, it will allow you to briefly experience the world as if the laws of physics don't apply to you personally.

Experiment with irrational beliefs. Perhaps blind faith comes easily for you. Perhaps it doesn't. Either way, you can push the limits by trying to make yourself believe in things that you know couldn't possibly be true: The earth is flat. The moon is made of cheese. The queen of England is your best friend. Can you trick your mind into believing these things, for just a few seconds? Notice how your mind reacts when you try.

Become a debunker. Debunking is a great way to enhance your sense of superiority over others. But many of the best subjects for debunking have already been taken. UFO sightings, Bigfoot, ESP . . . they've all been debunked before. So for a real challenge, try using a controversial subject on which you have a strongly held belief: That global warming is or is not caused by human activity. Or that God does or does not exist. How far can you get in debunking your own belief?

Further Reading: Books on Levitation, Magic, and the Art of Debunking

- Thomas Gilovich, *How We Know What Isn't So: The Fallibility of Human Reason in Everyday Life*, Free Press, 1993.
- Joshua Jay, *Magic: The Complete Course*, Workman Publishing, 2008.
- Jim Ottaviani, *Levitation: Physics and Psychology in the Service of Deception*, G. T. Labs, 2007.
- James Randi, *Flim-Flam!: Psychics, ESP, Unicorns, and Other Delusions*, Prometheus Books, 1982.
- Steve Richards, *Levitation: What It Is, How It Works, How to Do It*, Borgo Press, 1986.
- Michael Shermer, *Why People Believe Weird Things: Pseudoscience, Superstition, and Other Confusions of Our Time*, Holt, 2002.
- Mark Anthony Wilson, *Mark Wilson's Complete Course in Magic*, Running Press Kids, 2002.

30

Look Around

I am possibly one of the most visually challenged people on the planet. I struggle to notice or retain even the most obvious pieces of visual information. (What was my wife wearing when she walked through the room a minute ago? I honestly have no clue.) Is it simply that I'm not paying attention? Or is the way my mind processes sensory information inherently biased away from the visual domain? Explore the flexibility (or lack thereof) of your own sensory apparatus in an exercise designed to force your mind temporarily into a fully visual state of being.

What You'll Need
- A space to explore
- Earplugs

How to Do It
1. **Choose a space.** Consider your innate visual temperament in making the choice. If you tend to have a

hard time retaining visual information, a familiar space will yield the most interesting results. If you are an inherently visual person, consider choosing an unfamiliar place to do the exercise.

2. **Turn off your other senses.** Because your senses are autonomic functions, it is not actually possible to intentionally shut them down. So this will be an act of willpower and imagination. Start by putting in the earplugs. Move on to your sense of taste: Swallow any saliva in your mouth; then round your cheeks and hold your tongue in the open cavity of your mouth. Don't let it touch any part of your mouth. (You'll periodically have to swallow; that's okay.) Now erase your sense of smell by breathing through your mouth as you pinch your nose shut. Finally, imagine that the surface of your skin has suddenly gone numb.

3. **Look around.** Now shift your focus to your sense of sight. Begin by looking around casually, the way you would ordinarily take in your surroundings. Then make yourself pay attention to whatever it is that you don't notice when you only look casually. The level of detail here will vary greatly from person to person. Those who are innately visually oriented might have to go into intense levels of detail (the specific pattern on the fabric of the chair in front of you; the number of leaves on a particular branch). For those who are not

visually oriented, the details will be much more basic. Find the level of detail that feels challenging to you and focus there.

4. **Hold the image in your mind.** Close your eyes and try to hold in your mind a visual image of the place. Again, this experience will vary significantly depending on your innate visual style. As you hold the image, notice whether it starts to fade or whether it is essentially static, like a photograph. If it fades or changes, what does that tell you about what is changing and how?

5. **Open your eyes and turn your senses back on.** Look again at reality. How does the image in front of you differ from what you were holding in your mind? Perhaps it's just a difference in intensity or vividness. Perhaps small details are inaccurate. Or perhaps your mind has completely altered some parts of the image. Whatever the case, just notice it. Finally, reversing the process in step 2, turn your senses back on and go about your day.

Intuitive Seeing

Here's the funny thing: Although I can't tell you what my wife was wearing when she walked through the room a few minutes ago, I can still describe it in great detail. I can tell you that she was looking assertive, seeming "flowy" on the surface and well armored underneath. I could go on and on with these sorts of impressions, and I am certain that they would be a really good description of what she was wearing, even though there wouldn't be a single visual clue in that description.

This brings me to the Myers-Briggs Type Indicator (MBTI). This is a classic psychological test, based on some of the theoretical ideas of Carl Jung, that rates our personalities on four different scales. Are you an introvert or an extrovert? Are you more of a "thinking" person or a "feeling" person? Or, in the case at hand, are you more of a "sensing" person or an "intuiting" person? People who are high on the sensing scale will look at an object and take it in through their senses. Visually, their minds operate sort of like a camera. On the other hand, people who are high on the "intuition" scale will tend to draw information more from interior sources. They will know how an object makes them feel, and they'll be able to provide descriptions of the object that bring it vividly to life without ever describing it objectively.

Which is the more accurate description? Although it's easy to argue over this, the beauty of the MBTI is that it is absolutely nonjudgmental about where you fall on any of its scales. Neither side is bad nor good; they're simply descriptive of *types* of psychological approaches to the world.

Variations: Messing with Your Mind

What's your type? Take the MBTI or its close relative, the Keirsey Temperament Sorter, either on paper or online. Then have fun learning all about your type. If you really want to make it useful, have people you're close to take the test as well and learn about *their* type. Then sit back and watch as new, more constructive ways of interacting begin to emerge. (I'm INFJ, by the way. Can you use that information to help you make sense of how and why I've written this book?)

Explore false memory. One of the things that this exercise can illustrate is how quickly our memory (visual or otherwise) can begin to shift once we lose contact with the original object or experience. And the more time has passed, the trickier this becomes. This becomes quite a controversial issue when we consider accusations of abuse that center around recovered memories. How do we distinguish between accurate and inaccurate memories? How do we define the truth when it applies to memory? The fact is that memory is faulty. You can explore this in your own memory simply by looking back at some of you familiar childhood photographs. Can you find the line between your actual memory of yourself in the picture and what you have created over the years based on that photograph? (For extra fun, talk to a sibling or a parent and ask them for their recollection of that moment.)

Then consider this: what does it mean to you if your memory isn't factually accurate?

Expand your concept of truth. Once you accept the fact that human memory is an inherently messy process, the whole concept of "truth" becomes problematic. A great way to explore this is to do a simple exercise with a partner. Identify an experience you recently shared together. Then write down separate detailed descriptions of what you experienced. When you compare notes, you'll notice that you agree on some things, but there will also be divergent details. Some of those might be easily resolvable; one of you will simply acknowledge that the memory was mistaken. But there will also be details that you disagree on. How do you figure out which version is "true"? In the absence of documentation, all you've got is two separate memories. Is it possible that they can be contradictory and still be true?

As a final step, read Mary McCarthy's fascinating memoir, *Memories of a Catholic Girlhood*, in which each section is followed by an addendum explaining that what she knows about the account she has just told must not be accurate. Try structuring one of your own childhood memories in this way. Start by telling it just as you hold it in memory. Then make a list of things that might not or could not be true. Ask yourself, "Does the fact that it can't be accurate make it any less *true*?"

Further Reading: Books on Vision, Memory, and the MBTI

- Rudolph Arnheim, *Visual Thinking*, University of California Press, 2004.
- Renee Baron, *What Type Am I?: The Myers-Briggs Type Indication Made Easy*, Penguin, 1998.
- Temple Grandin, *Thinking in Pictures: And Other Reports from My Life with Autism*, Vintage Books, 2006.
- Donald D. Hoffman, *Visual Intelligence: How We Create What We See*, W. W. Norton, 1998.
- Eric R. Kandel, *In Search of Memory: The Emergence of a New Science of Mind*, W. W. Norton, 2006.
- David Keirsey and Marilyn Bates, *Please Understand Me II: Temperament, Character, Intelligence*, Prometheus Nemesis, 1998.
- Mary McCarthy, *Memories of a Catholic Girlhood*, Mariner, 1985.
- Daniel L. Schacter, *Searching for Memory: The Brain, the Mind, and the Past*, BasicBooks, 1996.

31

Power Down

When is the power really off? We've been hearing a lot lately about the ghostly world of "phantom power drains," inhabited by "energy vampires" that operate in the nether land between power outlets and appliances. It turns out that it can be genuinely difficult to figure out when you've truly minimized the drain on your home's energy. The same is true of our bodies and our spirits. What does it mean to truly *rest*? Explore the symbolic extremes of this dilemma by focusing for a few minutes on reducing the power drain on both the human-made and natural energy sources around you.

What You'll Need
• A room in your house

How to Do It
1. **Listen to the energy of the room.** Start by tuning in to power in its most mundane sense: the electrical

energy that keeps everything running in your home. Energy in our lives often reveals itself in the form of white noise, so begin by simply listening. Buzzing, humming, hissing—it's all got a power source. Notice as much of it as you can.

2. **Turn it off.** Now locate the source of as many electrical devices as you can and turn the devices off. Start by switching them off, but don't stop there. Remember those power vampires: unplug everything from outlets.

3. **Listen again.** You'll probably become aware of new sources of power that you missed the first time. If they're easy to shut off, go ahead and turn them off. But it may turn out that they are deeper sources of energy that you can't easily access, like an apartment building's furnace. Or they might be coming from outside, like the rumble of a bus. Just notice these things, accept the limitations, and try to stay focused on the absence of energy in the room.

4. **Tune in to invisible energies.** Here's where it gets interesting, because energy is not just electricity that is wired into our homes. Energy is everywhere—in the photosynthesis of the plants on your windowsill, in the wind that's making the leaves rustle outside, and in the warmth of the sun against your skin; it's the gravity that holds you to the ground and it's the beating of your heart. With artificial sources of electricity

mostly shut down, tune in to the energy of the world itself. Identify every source of energy that you can and imagine what it would be like to shut each of them off for a few minutes. Imagine that the wind stops blowing and that the warmth of the sun dissipates. Imagine the gravitational pull between the planets disappearing. Finally, imagine your own life energy slowing to a halt. For just a few moments, let every-thing die. Does it feel frightening or simply restful? However you experience it, try to hold on to this vision for a minute or two.

5. **Reanimate the world.** When you're ready, start switching everything back on. Start with yourself. Bring your breath back fully and feel the blood in your veins. Wiggle your fingers and toes. Breathe. Then move on to the larger world. Switch gravity back on, reignite the sun, and set the wind in motion. Finally, start plugging in the electrical devices in your home and turning them back on. As you move through the rest of your day, see if you can keep some awareness about the energetic network that is always surrounding you.

Rest in Peace

This exercise is about temporarily creating a state of deep rest in which the energies flowing through us and around

us are temporarily halted, or at least slowed. The irony is that the deepest forms of rest, while ultimately life-sustaining, strongly resemble a temporary state of death. We are wired (to use an inherently *energetic* term) to repeat the entire life cycle in the rhythms of our daily life. Sleep itself mimics death, just as waking is a rebirth.

Variations: De-energize and Reenergize

Get back to nature. A simple variation on this exercise is just to eliminate human-generated energy sources. Leave your electronic devices behind and get yourself out into the woods—far enough out that the only sources of energy you experience are those of the natural world and your own body.

Get off the grid. So much of the aggravation we experience around energy consumption comes from the fact that we depend on others to deliver power to us, whether it's oil from the Middle East or natural gas from our local utility. But what if we stopped depending on others for our energy? Some people have figured out how to do it. Explore what it would take to live "off the grid," generating all your own energy, and for that matter, your food, water, and other necessities. You may not want to take it that far, but knowing it's an option can open up unexpected space in the way you think about energy in your life.

Further Reading: Books to Help You Get Off the Grid

- Dave Black, *Living Off the Grid: A Simple Guide to Creating and Maintaining a Self-Reliant Supply of Energy, Water, Shelter, and More*, Skyhorse Publishing, 2008.
- *The Complete Guide to Reducing Energy Costs*, Consumer Reports, 2006.
- Lori Ryker, *Off the Grid Homes: Case Studies for Sustainable Living*, Gibbs Smith, 2007.
- Christine Woodside, *The Homeowner's Guide to Energy Independence: Alternative Power Sources for the Average American*, Lyons Press, 2006.

32

Wait

When you were a child and you got upset, your mother may have told you to take a breath and count to ten. It's a decent way to force yourself to wait before acting. The goal, of course, is to allow the intense emotions of the moment to dissipate. But waiting can also be a powerful intensifier of emotions. Harness the full power of waiting by activating a desire that can be immediately satisfied, and holding yourself for a few minutes just at the edge of fulfillment without letting the intensity of the desire diminish at all.

What You'll Need
- A craving
- The means to satisfy it

How to Do It
1. **Choose an object of desire.** Keep it really simple, really basic, and make it immediately obtainable. The easiest choice is probably food. Pick a food that you

absolutely love and a moment when you're feeling extremely hungry. Other options might include urges to sleep when you're feeling really tired or to call a friend and share a bit of juicy gossip.

2. **Amplify the desire.** Start by focusing inward on your experience of the desire itself. If you're hungry, try to feel that hunger so intensely that it feels like you'll pass out if you don't eat something. Then turn your focus outward. If you've got a piece of chocolate in your hands, smell the candy, caress it, and imagine it melting in your mouth. If you want to call someone to share that bit of gossip, you might try dialing the number and hanging up before it starts to ring.

3. **Wait.** Now take a deep breath . . . and do nothing. Just wait. Your mind is probably going to want to start reasoning with you over *why* you're waiting, or possibly start bargaining with you over how long you have to wait before you can fulfill your desire. When these thoughts arise, simply try to notice them, and then send them on their way. There is no *reason* you are waiting. You are simply waiting. There is no set length of time you are going to wait. This is simply the moment you are living: empty waiting.

4. **Make a false start.** Slowly, mindfully, initiate the first step toward satisfying your desire. Lift the chocolate toward your mouth. Pick up the phone and start to

dial. Let yourself feel like you're going to go through with it. Then stop yourself. This should be a frustrating but manageable experience—you're setting your instinctual urges at odds with your conscious thoughts. Again, your mind might get all active, creating reasons why you should or should not be continuing to wait. But there's no reason. You're just waiting.

5. **Act.** Slowly, deliberately, fulfill your desire. As you do this, try to feel the experience as completely as possible. Notice not just the taste of the chocolate in your mouth but the pure feeling of having the desire itself be fulfilled. This is possible. Let the pleasure of fulfillment infuse your day.

Patience, Context, Intensity

The human desire for intensifying experience takes many forms, from theme parks to rock concerts to drug abuse. Intense experience, whether in the form of an adrenaline rush or an emotional release, perceptual immersion, or spiritual communion, is part of what helps us feel connected to the full scope of our humanity. So it's no surprise that everywhere we go, intense experiences are available for purchase.

But as this exercise demonstrates, the intensity of any experience is as much a function of our mental process as the event itself, sometimes even more so. The simple element of anticipation kindles our expectations and heightens our senses. (Why else is it that every rock concert in the history of rock concerts has started late?) And just as time can act as an intensifier, so can context. (Why else is it that the music playing before every rock concert is so generic and bland?)

There are two implications here. The first is that others can manipulate the perceived intensity of your experience, even against your will. The second is that you can regulate the intensity of your own experience, without having to resort to mind-altering substances or to activities that involve great risks. Intensity is a choice that you can make at every moment. It's simply a matter of changing your state of mind.

Variations: Waiting Games

Add a countdown clock. It can be as simple as an egg timer, or you can do a literal, out-loud countdown. Do the same exercise above, but add some sort of device or activity to measure the time you have to wait. How does making the waiting period measurable and explicit alter your experience of waiting?

Give yourself a time-out. Not because you've done anything wrong. Just because. Put yourself in a dull spot and set the egg timer to five minutes. Reflect on your actions until the timer rings. Then go on about your business.

Demand immediate gratification. Take this exercise in exactly the opposite direction and return to your primal infant state in which you have no capacity for delaying gratification. Choose a pleasurable activity that you can repeat endlessly and safely for a limited amount of time. Then take five minutes or so to engage in that activity without waiting, with no holds barred. It could involve food again. (Pick a fruit that you really like and eat a boxful of them.) Or it could be something as simple as rolling around on your bed. Here, you're substituting one sort of intensity for another. See if you can notice without judgment the difference in experience between waiting for something and diving into it immediately.

Beyond waiting—deep patience. There are many things that we wait for mostly unconsciously, and sometimes with little hope: maturity, personal transformation, social change. Sometimes it can seem that consciously waiting for such things would be unbearable. Think about the things that you are waiting for. Pick one and spend a few moments waiting for it actively and consciously. Feel free to tap your foot while you wait.

Further Reading: On Delaying Gratification

- Sue Monk Kidd, *When the Heart Waits: Spiritual Direction for Life's Sacred Questions*, HarperSanFrancisco, 2006.

- Joachim de Posada and Ellen Singer, *Don't Eat the Marshmallow—Yet!: The Secret to Sweet Success in Work and Life*, Berkley Books, 2005.

33

Develop a Conspiracy Theory

Just because a few people have taken it a little too far, paranoia has gotten a bad rap. In fact, paranoia can be a useful approach to the world. In small doses it gives us insight into the hidden assumptions that allow our daily lives to move smoothly along. Take a few moments to imagine that an ordinary, innocuous occurrence is actually guided by an unseen hand (toward an evil end, of course). Let the insidious idea that "things aren't really as they seem" briefly pull you into anxiety and paralysis.

What You'll Need
- An everyday occurrence
- Suspicion

How to Do It
1. **Choose something to get suspicious about.** Consider the things in your life that feel unquestionably positive but depend on an unseen network to function:

the postal carrier delivering your mail, the warm water that fills your bathtub, the music on your iPod.

2. **Consider what you know.** Let's use mail delivery as an example. You know that you put a letter in the mailbox and somehow it gets picked up and delivered to its recipient ... at least most of the time. And maybe you know a little bit about what happens in between. Perhaps you went on a field trip to the post office in elementary school and you watched those sorting machines that flipped through letters at an unbelievable speed, sorting out the ZIP codes. How could that machine possibly do that?

3. **Consider what you *don't* know.** Now here's the meat and potatoes of every good conspiracy theory: no matter how much about an occurrence can be explained, there are always some things that can't be. And even if an explanation seems to make sense, there's always room for alternative explanations. This is the fertile ground on which paranoia thrives. Take a few moments to magnify your ignorance.

4. **Get paranoid.** Go to work on a theory that will explain everything about the occurrence that you don't understand. Start with a small question, like "Why did the letter that usually takes two days to arrive take *three* this time?" Come up with an explanation that involves evil intent on someone's part. Then, keeping it within

the realm of the possible, start thinking big. It's not just any conspiracy; it's a *vast* conspiracy. It's not just any plan; it's a *master* plan. If the government is reading our mail, it's undoubtedly compiling a database of everything in our letters. Be sure to let emotion in. Let fear magnify the conspiracy. What if it's not just our *mail* that they're reading? What if they're developing ways to track our thoughts?

5. **Talk yourself down.** Conspiracy theories thrive because it's very difficult to prove that they're *not* true, even if they seem implausible. So if you've come up with a particularly good theory, it might be a bit difficult to get yourself back into reality. Take a few minutes to nudge yourself back into a calmer line of reasoning. Wherever you are, plant your feet on the ground and look out at the solid, familiar world around you. You really are safe.

Why Would Paranoia Evolve as a Human Trait?

It's like a startle response: if you have it over every little thing, it's exhausting and useless. But if you *don't* have it when that car is about to run you over, you're not going to get the surge of adrenaline you need to get out of the way and save your life. We need a certain degree of suspicion in order to survive as a species, because sometimes people really *are* concocting evil schemes.

Say you're Hitler and you have an actual plan for world domination that stands some chance of success. The best thing you've got going for you is people's natural inclination not to be paranoid. No one wants to believe that you could possibly be that crazy, which gives you a perfect cover for your evil schemes.

Variations: From Logic Unbound to Occam's Razor

Imagine a world *without* evil intention. It's not as easy as John Lennon made it sound.

Experiment with jealousy. When you get right down to it, jealousy is essentially a paranoid conspiracy theory operating on an interpersonal level. If you have a naturally jealous temperament, use caution with this variation (or consider skipping it altogether) because suspicion can spin out of control so quickly. But if you're not an inherently suspicious person, it can be interesting to try this exercise using a person in your life as the subject. Choose someone who has something you want—a coworker with a slightly higher status, a neighbor with a slightly nicer house. Create a conspiracy theory that explains that person's advantage in terms of a secret plan to make you feel inferior and to deprive you of the things you want. Then—please—bring yourself back to reality.

Practice Occam's razor. Paranoia is hard work. It takes a lot of energy to monitor so many unseen forces.

Return to your senses by practicing this principle, which states that the simplest explanation for any phenomenon is usually the best. Run through the conspiracy theories you have created in this exercise and apply Occam's razor to them: what's the simplest explanation that can account for the event? The clear downfall of many conspiracy theories, no matter how clever (especially if they're particularly clever) is their lack of parsimony. There is almost always a simpler explanation. And that simpler explanation is almost always the right one.

Further Reading: Books on Paranoia and Conspiracy

- Martin Kantor, *Understanding Paranoia: A Guide for Professionals, Families, and Sufferers*, Praeger, 2004.
- James McConnachie and Robin Tudge, *The Rough Guide to Conspiracy Theories*, Rough Guides, 2005.
- Daniel Pipes, *Conspiracy: How the Paranoid Style Flourishes and Where It Comes From*, Simon & Schuster, 1999.
- Brad Steiger and Sherry Steiger, *Conspiracies and Secret Societies: The Complete Dossier*, Visible Ink Press, 2006.
- Robert Anton Wilson with Miriam Joan Hill, *Everything Is Under Control: Conspiracies, Cults, and Cover-ups*, HarperCollins, 1998.

34

Set Up a Perimeter

You hear it in cop shows all the time: after a robbery, someone says, "We're setting up a ten-block perimeter around the area." The procedure of defining boundaries operates on many different levels: from national borders to local zoning, from private property to social distance, from mammalian territoriality to cellular microbiology. All boundaries are meant to do two opposite things at once: to keep some things out while letting others in. And, of course, we can experience them as either protective or restrictive. This exercise focuses your attention on the perimeters that you set up for yourself as you briefly establish an artificial boundary around your own movements.

What You'll Need
- A space that can be subdivided
- Masking tape or something else to mark a boundary

How to Do It

1. **Explore the space.** In whatever space you have chosen, there will be natural boundaries in place that you can use (or not) as you like—walls, doors, and so on. If this is a space you know well, try to see it from a new perspective so that you can divide it in arbitrary ways that have no inherent relationship to the preexisting arrangement of the structure.

2. **Choose the boundary you're going to set.** Everything rests on this, really. It can be extremely small—so small that you literally cannot move while remaining in it. Or it can be expansive. What will it include, and what will be excluded? If you're doing this exercise in your house, are you going to give yourself access to the kitchen, the front door, the stereo? All these choices are yours to make. Keep in mind that the exercise will be more interesting if you make the boundary lines seem arbitrary or even a little strange.

3. **Mark the boundaries and name the new country.** Define the boundary precisely, ideally with masking or painter's tape. You might consider leaving one portion as a "disputed area," with several competing boundary lines. This is your new country. Give it a name. Feel free to name it after yourself. After all, you are not only its sole inhabitant, but you are also its ruler.

4. **Explore the limits of this new territorial entity.**
My grandfather, a sheep rancher, called it "walking the fence." We'd make our way along the boundary of his property, checking the fence for gaps, making sure the No Trespassing signs hadn't been marred or stolen. Here you can focus on the *emotional* experience of this particular dividing line. What is within it? What is out of reach? What feelings does this awareness create? Experiment with standing at the edge of the boundary and seeing what you can reach on the other side.

5. **Bust out.** Consider the permeability of the border that you have just created. Can it be easily crossed, or would doing so entail great sacrifice and risk? It's entirely up to you. But no boundary is absolute, so even if you are imagining the most secure border possible, figure out what it would take to get across and do what is necessary to get onto the other side. Then do it. Finally, take a minute to "walk the fence" from the outside, exploring how this territory looks from there.

Personal Boundaries

What would a map of your own personal boundaries look like? As a therapist I spend a lot of time thinking about the quality of interpersonal boundaries. You've heard it said of someone that "she has very good boundaries" or that "he has no boundaries at all." But what exactly does

this mean? To me, healthy personal boundaries are a clear definition of one's self, knowing what one has to give and what one doesn't; what one is willing to do and what one isn't; what is negotiable and what isn't. So much angst and despair in relationships arise from a lack of clarity about these things. And so much of the nuts-and-bolts work of therapy comes down to figuring out what we are and are not willing to give and to receive from others, and (of course) why.

Variations: Extending the Boundary

Create a personal force field. Anthropologists talk about the concept of "social distance," the amount of space that *feels* right between two people as they interact. It's different in different cultures, which leads to some interesting dance steps during cross-cultural social events. As you interact with others, notice where your own social distance comfort is. Experiment with expanding and contracting that boundary beyond what feels inherently comfortable. Then imagine your social boundaries as an impermeable force field. Imagine your inner self alone, outside of any social constructs. How does the world look from the perspective of absolute isolation?

Experience constriction: design a prison. Some perimeters function almost entirely as vehicles of containment. Prisons, of course, are the most powerful symbols of such a system. Try to imagine what it would take to design a boundary so severe that once inside it becomes impossible to leave? How could life be maintained under such circumstances?

Experience oppression: territorial fences. Berlin, Mexico, Palestine. These are prison walls too, but we often see them only from the outside. Consider how keeping people *out* is in fact the same thing as keeping people *in*. Try to imagine the task that the designers of these huge border fences face: how do you build a perimeter around an entire people?

Feel no limits. Finally, try to contemplate a world without territorial boundaries of any kind. What fantasies, anxieties, or other feelings come to mind?

Further Reading: Books on Boundaries

- Avram S. Bornstein, *Crossing the Green Line Between the West Bank and Israel*, University of Pennsylvania Press, 2003.
- Rajiv Chandrasekaran, *Imperial Life in the Emerald City: Inside Iraq's Green Zone,* Vintage Books, 2007.
- David J. Danelo, *The Border: Exploring the U.S.-Mexican Divide*, Stackpole Books, 2008.
- Leslie Fairweather and Sean McConville, *Prison Architecture: Policy, Design and Experience*, Architectural Press, 2000.

- Norman Johnston, *Forms of Constraint: A History of Prison Architecture*, University of Illinois Press, 2000.
- Anne Katherine, *Boundaries: Where You End and I Begin*, Simon & Schuster, 1993.
- Charles L. Whitfield, *Boundaries and Relationships: Knowing, Protecting, and Enjoying the Self*, Health Communications, 1993.

35

Define Your Terms

You know those people who keep interrupting you during an argument, asking you to explain what *exactly* you mean by a certain word or phrase? In this exercise you will become that person to yourself as you make a to-do list and then interact with the list as if it were an adversary in an argument, forcing yourself to define your terms as precisely as possible. Watch how quickly the precision of definition descends into the chaos of relativity, and how your focus on the future narrows to the present moment.

What You'll Need
- A writing pad
- A pencil

How to Do It
1. **Make your to-do list.** Most of the exercises in this book are aimed at bringing you into a clearer awareness of the present moment. But in *this* step of *this* exercise,

you get to focus on the future. Do this by quickly making a list of things you need to do in the next twenty-four hours, more or less in the order they need to be done. Nothing fancy here—just the nuts and bolts of your life.

2. **Fully and explicitly define the first item on your list.** Let me illustrate using my list, at this very moment, which begins: go to the gym, do the grocery shopping, prepare for my clients. Placing my list on the witness stand, I ask it, "What exactly to do you mean by 'go to the gym'?" Take the first item on your list and write a detailed answer to this question. In my case I might write, "I change into my gym clothes, get in the car, drive over to the gym, and work out."

3. **Pick a word or phrase from the definition and interrogate it.** Stay in the role of the (slightly insane) prosecuting attorney. Pick a word or phrase from the beginning of the definition you've just written and demand further definition. Feel free to select a word or phrase that strikes you as particularly interesting. For instance, "You say, 'I change into my gym clothes.' I wonder if you can tell me exactly what you mean by the words 'I change.'" Then write out your response. You'll notice that things start to get a little strange at this point. That's fine. Just go with it.

4. **Give the second, third, and fourth meanings of the term.** Here, imagine the prosecuting attorney lis-

tening to your definition in step 3 and saying something like, "True enough, but aren't there *other* meanings as well?" Force yourself to come up with at least four separate definitions.

5. **Repeat. Take the first definition you created and interrogate it using the same process.** Definition is an endlessly recursive activity. That's to say that it's an action that can be repeatedly reapplied to itself. Ordinarily we draw artificial lines to stop this process of recursion and to create an (illusory) sense of order in our chaotic lives. So how will you know when are you done with this exercise? Simple: Give it ten minutes. Wherever you are in the process of definition, let it stand.

But Why?

You're absolutely right to ask that question. In fact, this exercise is very much indeed like the four-year-old practice of asking a question and then repeatedly asking "Why?" no matter what the answer is. There is no solid ending point, no way to escape the endless definitional loops. As with measurement (see exercise 23, Make a List, for a further discussion of this subject), the art of definition involves defining acceptable levels of precision for the task at hand. Just as you can always identify more precise units of measurement, you can also always create a more detailed and precise definition of a term by further

defining the definition itself. But, of course, greater definition comes at a cost. There is always a certain point at which the *amount* of data begins to obscure the *meaning* of that information. So why do this exercise? To reawaken ourselves to the simple truth that we first figured out when we were four years old: that words can only be defined in terms of other words; that clearly defined terms mask endless recursive processes.

Variations: High-Definition

Read definitions in the dictionary. It's easy to start doing this. But the challenge, I find, is to *actually* read full definitions. When we do this, a natural urgency kicks in. We want to find out what's next. Or we want to find a really interesting word instead of going into so much detail about the boring one you happened to open to. Try reading a few definitions in their entirety. Can you sustain your focus?

Write your own dictionary. It's incredible how much mental energy is required to write a good definition of an ordinary word from scratch. Try it, using a few ordinary nouns, verbs, and adjectives. Try *table*, for instance (the noun has sixteen meanings in the *American Heritage Dictionary*). When you're done, compare your definitions to those in an actual dictionary. Better yet, compare them to the definitions in several different dictionaries.

Write a fake dictionary. Engage in a perennial favorite activity of older siblings all over the world: write devious redefinitions of ordinary words. To get the most out of this variation, make sure that your definitions are designed to get anyone who uses them into trouble.

Further Reading: Books on Definitions

- Henry Hitchings, *Defining the World: The Extraordinary Story of Dr. Johnson's Dictionary*, Farrar, Straus and Giroux, 2005.
- K. M. Elisabeth Murray, *Caught in the Web of Words: James A. H. Murray and the Oxford English Dictionary*, Yale University Press, 2001.
- Ammon Shea, *Reading the OED: One Man, One Year, 21,730 Pages*, Perigee Trade, 2008.
- J. A. Simpson and E. S. C. Weiner, eds., *The Oxford English Dictionary*, Oxford University Press, 1989.
- Simon Winchester, *The Meaning of Everything: The Story of the Oxford English Dictionary*, Oxford University Press, 2003.
- Simon Winchester, *The Professor and the Madman: A Tale of Murder, Insanity, and the Making of the Oxford English Dictionary*, HarperPerennial, 2005.

36

Plug Your Ears

What's the best thing to do when someone starts telling you something you don't want to hear? Plug your ears, of course. But while you might be able to block out someone's voice, you can't stop yourself from hearing the inner workings of your own body. Explore the fuzzy line between external stimuli and internally generated sensations by plugging your ears as completely as possible. How little sound is it possible to hear? And how much noise is present inside you when you block out everything that comes from the outside?

What You'll Need
- Your ears
- Two fingers

How to Do It
1. **Pick a spot.** While the choice of location will have a significant effect on how you experience this exercise,

it will work well whether you do it on a busy subway platform or in an abandoned warehouse. The choice is purely a matter of personal preference. Less external noise will heighten your awareness of your "internal" noise; more external noise will heighten your awareness of the omnipresent intrusion of sound into your internal experience.

2. **Listen outwardly, listen inwardly.** Begin by simply listening to all the sounds you can hear around you, whatever they might be. Then see if you can—without covering your ears yet—make yourself aware of any sounds coming from inside your own body. This is extremely difficult to do, but give it a try.

3. **Plug your ears.** Choose a finger on each hand and place it over the opening of each ear, applying enough pressure to block out external sounds as much as possible. Feel free to rest your hands on your cheeks, if that feels comfortable. Notice the instant and dramatic shift in sound. What remains of the external noises you noticed earlier? And what new sounds are created by the act of covering your ears? (You might be wondering why I don't want you to use earplugs. The reason is that I want you to be able to regulate the amount of pressure you put on your ears, which keeps the activity *intentional* and makes it more difficult for your awareness to drift during the exercise.)

4. **Keep them covered.** This is more difficult than it sounds. It's easy to get a quick first impression of changes in tones and sounds when you plug up your ears. But this step involves listening to rhythms within the rumbling sounds of your inner ears and enhancing your awareness of the many sources of sound that can't be easily erased, like your breathing and the small movements of the joints of your fingers. To heighten the effect, consider closing your eyes. You will notice your thoughts wandering. Try to keep bringing them back to the sensation of sound.

5. **Unplug.** But be sure to do this mindfully, because it's the best part of the exercise. You have two choices here: unplug gradual or unplug quick. Each has its advantages. Unplugging your ears gradually will allow the range of sound frequencies to slowly increase until your ears are fully open again; this makes it easier to appreciate the experience. Doing it quickly makes mindfulness of the experience more challenging, but it also heightens the change in sensation. Either way, try to catch that initial moment of change, to magnify your awareness of what happens in that split second. How much have you not been hearing? And how long can you keep hearing these sounds before you lose your awareness of them again?

Un-Silent Silence

Back in the early eighties, I attended a performance by the Philip Glass Ensemble that dramatically affected my appreciation of the relationship between silence and sound. The pieces were performed by a group of organs, woodwinds, and vocalists, and they swirled repetitively in hypnotically shifting patterns. The music was *loud*, and because of the repetitive structure of the compositions, there was no way to tell how long each piece was going to be. So it was a surprise when each piece ended, and the acoustic effect was incredible: a wall of sound was suddenly replaced by absolute silence. But you didn't experience the silence as *silence*. The absence of noise was like a physical sensation, a push of energy that rushed in to fill the vacuum left by the abrupt cessation of the music. To me, it was an ecstatic experience. It was as if the sound made by the inside of my soul was suddenly revealed to me. But then, much too quickly for me, the audience rushed in to applaud the performance. I wanted them to stop. I wanted to stand up and make a speech: "Listen to what happens when the music ends. Listen to that un-silent silence. It's as magical and revelatory as a solar eclipse. During an eclipse, the illusion of daylight is briefly pulled back, and our larger place in the dark universe is revealed. And when silence is made

palpable like this, we are allowed to experience, for just a moment, the sonic architecture hidden beneath the white noise of everyday life."

Variations: Good Vibrations

Sing. Do this exercise as if someone were trying to tell you things you didn't want to hear. Try to block out their voice by singing "La la la la la" as loud as you can while covering your ears. As you do this, pretend not to hear anything at all while paying close attention to the sound of your own voice heard through closed ears.

Feel the vibration. The previous variation makes use of the fact that sounds are simply vibrations, which means that we don't depend entirely on our ears for hearing. When you feel the vibration of the rap beat from the subwoofer in a car passing your house, that's your body "hearing" frequencies so low that your ears wouldn't pick them up on their own. Experiment with doing this exercise, focusing on vibration rather than sound.

Go underwater. Immersing our heads in water creates much the same sensation as simply plugging our ears, except that instead of hearing the joints in your fingers move, you hear the vibrations that are carried through the water. Try a shortened version of this exercise in the bathtub or a swimming pool. Or extend your time underwater by doing the exercise using a snorkel.

Know noise. What is noise, really? It sounds simple, but it's actually quite difficult to define. Try this exercise again, focusing on this simple question: *Is what I'm hearing noise or not?*

Further Reading: Books on Sound and Noise

- Richard E. Berg and David G. Stork, *The Physics of Sound*, Benjamin Cummings, 2005.
- John Cage, *Silence: Lectures and Writings*, Wesleyan University Press, 1961.
- Simon Cann, *How to Make a Noise: A Comprehensive Guide to Synthesizer Programming*, Coombe Hill Publishing, 2007.
- George Michelsen Foy, *Zero Decibels: The Quest for Absolute Silence*, Scribner, 2010.
- Don Ihde, *Listening and Voice: Phenomenologies of Sound*, State University of New York Press, 2007.
- Garret Keizer, *The Unwanted Sound of Everything We Want: A Book About Noise*, Public Affairs, 2010.
- Bart Kosko, *Noise*, Viking, 2006.
- George Prochnik, *In Pursuit of Silence: Listening for Meaning in a World of Noise*, Doubleday, 2010.

37

Write a Letter

Now, I'm no Luddite. I write and compose music on computers, I communicate mostly through email, and I think that most new technology is inherently cool. But there's still this little part of my brain that nags at me about what we lose when all our communication becomes instantaneous and digital. The physical act of writing a letter slows us down enough to remember what a moment of communication really feels like.

What You'll Need
- A message and a recipient
- A pen and paper
- An envelope and a stamp

How to Do It
1. **Choose a message and a recipient.** There are two ways to approach this exercise. The first is to identify a message that you need to communicate anyway, and

then write it in a letter rather than using whatever method you would ordinarily use. The second is to write a letter to someone for no particular reason at all. Either one will work, but each will yield a slightly different experience. Whichever you choose, try to keep it simple. Limit it to something that you can express in a paragraph or two. Think positive (it will be more fun that way), think short, and make it something that doesn't need to be received in the next ten minutes.

2. **Do a mental rough draft.** Yes, I'm going to make you do this, not because I get a thrill out of pretending to be your high school English teacher, but because the whole point here is to slow down and experience the process. So write the whole thing in your mind before you commit it to paper. As you do this, notice how you revise your words in your mind before you've even started writing. Take the time to figure out the most concise and elegant way to say what you need to say so that you don't have to apologize, as Pascal famously did: "The present letter is a very long one, simply because I had no time to make it shorter" (2007, 571).

3. **Write it down.** Can you feel the scrape of your pen against the paper? That's friction. Let that sensation blossom into a feeling of frustration (*it doesn't have to take this long*). Then see if you can transform that frustration. Can

you experience it not as an impediment but as a feeling of heightened anticipation?

4. **Seal the deal.** When you're done writing, reread your letter. Then put it into an envelope. Address the envelope and include the return address. Do this all by hand—no labels allowed!—and do it neatly, the way you were taught in fifth grade. Moisten the edge of the envelope, seal it, and apply the correct postage.

5. **Wait.** Set the letter down in front of you and look at it. Appreciate the lovely physical object that it is. Think about the feeling, the small thrill you still get when you receive a personal letter in the mail. Know that you are giving this to someone else. Finally, before you put the letter in the mailbox, let yourself be aware of how this exercise ends on a frustrating pause. It will be two, three, or even four days before your letter reaches its destination. As you move through those days, try from time to time to remind yourself of this frustrating delay, trying each time to transform frustration into a feeling of anticipation.

Reflective Functioning

As anyone who's ever written even just a few words in a journal or diary knows, writing down a thought changes your relationship to that thought. And writing a note or a letter to another person changes how you experience your relationship to that person. These changes occur because we *externalize* our experience. When we read our own thoughts on paper, we see ourselves not just from our habitual subjective perspective but also from the outside. Psychologists call this capacity to observe our own thoughts and behavior "reflective functioning," and it is an absolutely essential foundation for good mental health and maturity. Reflective functioning gives us the capacity to not just feel our immediate experience but to simultaneously make sense of that experience. There are many ways of being and many states of mind that can help strengthen our capacity for reflective functioning (in fact, each of the exercises in this book strives to do just that). But one of the best ways to enhance this ability in yourself is the simple act of writing down your thoughts.

Variations: Correspondence Courses

Pass notes. Get even more concise by practicing the art of written notes. Your spouse, your children, or other loved ones are the obvious first choice of recipients. Use small pieces of paper (Post-it notes are fine) and find ways to make a connection in the fewest words possible.

Write a letter you'll never send. It's a classic technique that still works beautifully. Think of someone you're angry with and write a letter to them in which you really

let loose. Rip them a new one, as it were. Write everything you feel, especially the things you know you would later regret having written. If you want to heighten the sensation, put the letter in an envelope (you can even put a stamp on it if you want) and let it sit around for a few days before you destroy it. Or just tear it up right now.

Write a letter to someone who can't read it. When our first son turned one, my wife wrote him a letter. In it, she simply described who he was and who we were at that moment in time. Now when she gets it out and reads it to our 13-year-old son, he listens raptly, and she and I are instantly in tears. An equally powerful exercise is to write a letter to someone who has gone out of your life for some reason. If someone has hurt you or you have hurt someone, if you've lost someone you still long for, write to them and let the relationship come alive within you.

Further Reading: Books of Letters

- Lester J. Cappon, ed., *The Adams-Jefferson Letters: The Complete Correspondence Between Thomas Jefferson and Abigail and John Adams*, University of North Carolina Press, 1988.
- Andrew Carroll, ed., *War Letters: Extraordinary Correspondence from American Wars*, Washington Square Press, 2001.

- Lisa Grunwald and Stephen J. Adler, eds., *Letters of the Century: America 1900–1999*, Dial Press, 1999.
- Lisa Grunwald and Stephen J. Adler, eds., *Women's Letters: America from the Revolutionary War to the Present*, Dial Press, 2005.
- Margaret A. Hogan and C. James Taylor, ed., *My Dearest Friend: Letters of Abigail and John Adams*, Belknap Press, 2007.
- Blaise Pascal, *Pensées: The Provincial Letters*, Becker Press, 2007.

38

Decide

Homicide, suicide, decide: Etymologically, a sort of death is embedded within every decision we make. It's the death of options not chosen. Take a few minutes to focus your attention on the act of deciding by bringing full awareness to the small physical decisions that usually happen unconsciously, like crossing your legs, stretching, and blinking. Experience these small movements as conscious choices and allow yourself to become aware of the paths you have chosen not to follow at any given moment.

What You'll Need
• Your body

How to Do It
1. **Keep still.** Start by sitting as still as possible in a chair. Keep your arms by your side, your legs uncrossed, your eyes open, and your head facing forward. Breathe normally. As you sit, try to notice everything that your

body is doing without making a conscious decision to do it. You'll notice your breathing, of course. But there's more. Are your eyes scanning the room? Are any of your muscles clenching? Is your tongue moving inside your mouth? Are you swallowing? Take a few minutes and notice all of it.

2. **Choose an action.** Focus your mind on some small, discreet action that has a definite beginning and an end—let's say, crossing your legs. Think about taking this action, but don't do it yet. Remind yourself that you could still cross them or not.

3. **Contemplate acting ... and not acting.** Before you decide to act, notice what it feels like *not* to act. There's a good chance that in refraining from acting you'll feel a strong urge to perform the action that you are contemplating. Notice that urge and see what happens if you simply stay aware of it without acting on it. Take a few minutes here to really sink into the pre-decision awareness. What you are feeling now is what you will lose, however briefly, once you decide to act.

4. **Decide to do it.** Commit to taking action.

5. **Act.** Or surprise yourself by *changing* your mind at the last minute and deciding not to act. If you decide to act, move slowly, trying to maintain awareness of both the physical action of your body and the mental act of deciding. Try to make every bit of movement intentional.

If you have decided not to act, the same principles apply, because stillness is also a decision.

Intention versus Decision

As anyone who has ever struggled with addictive behaviors will tell you, the decision to change is very different than the act of changing. So what *is* a decision, really? To get at this question, we need to draw a distinction between intentions and decisions. Often we speak of our intentions as if they were decisions, but in fact they are quite different. Intention precedes decision, but it is not sufficient to motivate us to action. Intention is the will to move in a certain direction. It is not a commitment to do so.

Consider the example of New Year's resolutions. We think of these as decisions. We have decided that we will work out more often or spend more time with our children. In fact, these are simply intentions. They are stories we tell ourselves about the sort of people we want to be. So it shouldn't be too surprising that New Year's resolutions rarely hold, or that addicts relapse, or that we almost always gain back weight we manage to lose on a diet. Transforming an intention into a real decision is truly hard work.

Variations: Decisions, Decisions . . .

Try to experience everything as a decision. Return to step 1 of the exercise, to the awareness of all the

involuntary activity that is happening in your body all the time. How much of it can you make intentional? Narrate this mentally. Tell yourself: Inhale. Wait. Exhale. Or: Blink. Look to the left. Blink again.

Contemplate impossible decisions. This is a variation of the ever-popular "Would You Rather" game, in which you are asked to make impossible or nonsensical choices. Choices can be either positive (Would you rather be able to fly or to be invisible?) or negative (Would you rather lose an arm or a leg?). If you find the choice to be too easy, keep fine-tuning the options until you arrive at a decision so agonizing that you are paralyzed by indecision.

Accept when there's no right decision. Write a list of decisions that you've had to make in your life in which it felt like everything was at stake and there was no clear way to decide. Can you feel again the tension underlying those decisions? What emotions are attached to that energy? Pick one such decision and see if you can find a way to express the intensity of that dilemma creatively, in writing, art, or music.

Grieve. The simple truth is that every decision—even a positive one—involves losses. And losses need to be grieved. Think about a decision that you've made in your life that you feel good about, something that you feel with certainty was the right decision to make. Then let

yourself consider the path not taken. What did you give up in making that decision? Try to feel what you have lost, and then to let it go.

Further Reading: Books on Decision Making

- Jonathan Baron, *Thinking and Deciding*, Cambridge, 4th ed., University Press, 2008.
- Scott de Marchi and James T. Hamilton, *You Are What You Choose: The Habits of Mind that Really Determine How We Make Decisions*, Portfolio, 2009.
- Reid Hastie and Robin M. Dawes, *Rational Choice in an Uncertain World: The Psychology of Judgment and Decision Making*, Sage Publications, 2010.
- Justin Heimberg and David Gomberg, *Would You Rather . . . ?: Over 200 Absolutely Absurd Dilemmas to Ponder*, Plume, 1997.
- Jonah Lehrer, *How We Decide*, Houghton Mifflin Harcourt, 2009.
- Scott Plous, *The Psychology of Judgment and Decision Making*, McGraw-Hill, 1993.

39

Surrender

When things in our lives get really hard, we all sometimes fantasize about just giving up. But in truth, fully surrendering is difficult to do. It goes against our basic survival instincts. Take a few minutes to pretend that you have no hope in achieving an important life goal. Will you experience this surrender as a loss of power or as liberation?

What You'll Need
- A long-term goal
- A piece of white cloth

How to Do It
1. **Make a quick list of your long-term goals.** Make sure that they're things that don't come easily, like writing a novel, buying a house, or taking early retirement. When you're done, look over your list. Which of your goals feels most urgent?

2. **Cling.** Take the goal you identified in step 1 and let yourself feel all the reasons you want it to come true. How long have you known that you wanted it? What are all the ways that you've been trying to reach this goal? How far would you go to achieve it? What do you tell yourself will happen if you can't have it?

3. **Check out the opposition.** Make a mental list of all the forces that stand in the way of you achieving your goal—money, influence, luck, motivation, whatever. Picture these forces as enemy troops in a war movie. They've got their guns pointed at you. They outnumber you, and they're far stronger than you. They have you nearly surrounded. Feel the contrast between the intensity of your desire and the negative energy opposing you.

4. **Abandon hope.** We're all wired differently when it comes to surrender, so everyone is going to have a different experience of this step. But whether you're an optimist or a pessimist, whether your motto is Never Say Never or Shit Happens, the challenge here is the same: to let yourself experience a feeling of true hopelessness. It will probably help—I'm serious here—if you lie down on your stomach on the floor. Imagine the enemy troops all standing over you. Try to let the energy go out of your body. Surrender to gravity itself. Then take that sensation and apply it to your goal. Tell yourself, "It's never going to happen."

5. **Raise the white flag.** While continuing to meditate on the unattainable goal, get up slowly from the floor, holding the white cloth and raising both your hands. Take several steps forward, into the imaginary enemy camp, and then get down on your knees, keeping your hands in the air, eyes facing downward. Stay in this position for several minutes. Let yourself experience *everything* that comes up. How many different emotions can you identify? Anger? Frustration? Grief? Resistance? Relief? That last one should be in the mix. See if you can locate it; then release yourself into a stance of non-struggle. Rest in that state for a few moments before getting up. When you're ready, get up, shake out your entire body vigorously, and then go about your day. The exercise is over now. No need to dwell on it.

Hope, Power, Surrender

How much power do you tell yourself you have?

I'm guessing that whatever your answer is to this question, it's not a very accurate assessment. Most of us either overstate or understate our personal power. We overstate it as a calculated bluff to give us more influence and safety as we move through the world. Or we understate it for essentially the same reasons. Some of us do both, depending on the situation. It's often in our interest to manipulate other people's perceptions of our personal power.

The complication is that we're not just deceiving others; we also fool ourselves.

The act of surrendering is powerful because it calls our bluff. In order to truly surrender, we need to acknowledge our *actual* power in the world. And often this requires us to reorganize our concept of our self. This is why *surrender* is such a complicated word, filled with paradoxical connotations. It is about giving up power, but it is also about safety and relief. To those who have experienced interpersonal trauma in the past, it's likely to evoke enslavement. For those who have experienced sustained, deep love, it can evoke profound acceptance.

Variations: Giving In

Play the enemy. Take your inner bad guy (we've all got one) out for a quick, imaginary joyride. Imagine that you are entirely in control over the fulfillment of another person's wishes. Then create an imaginary scenario in which the other person comes to you seeking permission to do something. It is your job to crush their every hope of ever doing this thing. How are you doing to go about it? You might find that it's not easy to crush hope from the outside.

Exaggerate disinterest. No matter how provocative an issue seems, there will always be *someone* out there who finds it utterly uninteresting. What this means for you is that it's theoretically possible to experience our most passionate needs and desires with neutrality and objectivity. Try it, using the list of goals you generated earlier. For each of them, imagine a person for whom that goal would be utterly meaningless. Then try to see that goal from that person's perspective.

Accept. Begin this breathing exercise by taking a few moments just to notice the natural movement of your breathing. Then, when you're ready, pause for a moment at the end of your next exhalation and say to yourself, "I accept" before you inhale again. Don't add any other words; just let the phrase resonate as broadly and as powerfully as possible. Surrender to what is, and feel the freedom.

Further Reading: Books on Hopelessness and Surrender

- Russ Harris, *The Happiness Trap: How to Stop Struggling and Start Living*, Trumpeter, 2008.
- Iris Krasnow, *Surrendering to Yourself: You Are Your Own Soul Mate*, Miramax Books/Hyperion, 2003.
- Paul Watzlawick, *The Situation Is Hopeless But Not Serious (The Pursuit of Unhappiness)*, W. W. Norton, 1993.

40

Interrupt Yourself

The word *interruption* has mostly negative connotations, but there's nothing inherently negative about breaks and ruptures. It all depends on what is being interrupted. For instance, the ability to interrupt negative or counterproductive thoughts is extremely useful. Take a few minutes to strengthen your control over your own thoughts by purposefully interrupting every idea that comes into your head.

What You'll Need
- Access to your thoughts

How to Do It
1. **Choose an interruption.** Keep it simple: "Excuse me ...," "Just a sec ...," "Hold it ..." All you need is a quick phrase with no content, a simple request for your attention.
2. **Watch your thoughts.** Before you start interrupting yourself, just notice whatever happens to be going

through your mind at this moment without acting on it in any way. Allow any thoughts that occur to you to flow effortlessly through your mind.

3. **Enter the interrupter.** You'll notice that in step 2 you split your mind into two parts: the thinking self and the observing self. Now you're going to create a third mental state: the interrupter. To help you keep track of who's who, you might create a persona for this voice. Maybe there's someone in your life who always does interrupt you. Or maybe you'd rather start from scratch and imagine the sort of person who would incessantly use your chosen interruption.

4. **Break in on yourself.** Let your observing ego play the role of stage manager here. As it notices you thinking about something, let it cue the interrupter. Imagine him walking in, stating the interruption—"Excuse me . . ."— and then just standing there maddeningly. Feel the frustrating pause, and then wait for the next thought to arise. As you do this, resist the temptation to simply repeat the interruption over and over again. The point here is to experience the actual moment of interruption. In order to do this, you have to give your mind room enough to wander. (Don't worry; it will.)

5. **Repeat.** It will probably take a little while to get the hang of this; it's more difficult than it seems. Stay with it for as long as you can, but don't worry if you don't

last as long as you'd like. At the moment when you give up, you'll have gotten the point.

Hearing Voices

Some people resist the idea that their mind is made up of competing "voices." It just sounds so *schizophrenic*. But we all intuitively recognize that this is how our minds work. We recognize it when we "argue with ourselves," when we play devil's advocate, or when we try to see things from another person's perspective. In fact, this quality is what makes empathy possible at all.

But it's also true that these "voices" (I prefer the term *ego states*) can be problematic as well. This is probably most evident in the voice of the "inner critic." We all have some version of this, the nagging voice that talks us down and tells us all sorts of bad things about ourselves. Worse yet is the experience of those whose lives have been shattered by trauma so severe that it became necessary to split off awareness of that event from the rest of their experiences.

But for the most part, these voices simply represent different aspects of ourselves. They're always accessible. You can watch them drifting in and out of your thoughts. There's my nine-year-old self. There's my inner adolescent. There I am as an infant. With the help of a solid enough container provided by a strong, "observing ego," these ego states reveal us to ourselves.

Variations: We Interrupt This Broadcast ...

Jam the signal. Let yourself do what I specifically asked you *not* to do in step 4 of the exercise: repeat your interruption constantly. Turn everything inside out and see if you can repeat an interruption so forcefully and continuously that you block out any thought before it can arise.

Concentrate. Take the exercise in just the opposite direction and try to stomp out unintentional cognitive interruptions as they arise. Choose an inherently difficult subject to think about. (The origins of the universe, say.) Try to concentrate exclusively on exploring that topic for ten minutes. The interruptions that arise will probably be much more tempting than the meaningless one you came up with earlier for this exercise. They'll come in the forms of worry or desire. They'll come to you with sad puppy eyes and beg for your attention or, like playground bullies, demand it. See if you can use the power of your observing ego to gently set these interruptions aside. If you want, you can promise yourself that you'll get back to them later, because you know that they're not going away.

Wait for it. We think of an interruption as a negative thing mostly because we think of it as something that blocks us from pleasure. But as any good storyteller knows, even an interruption to a pleasurable activity can be a positive thing. A pause before the resolution of a dramatic conflict heightens the tension and intensifies our pleasure in the resolution. As you go through your day, notice all the small moments of pleasure and satisfaction that you experience. See if you can get yourself to pause, for just the briefest moment, before fulfilling these desires.

Further Reading: Books on Ego States and Self-Talk

- Dr. Pamela Butler, *Talking to Yourself: How Cognitive Behavior Therapy Can Change Your Life*, BookSurge, 2008.
- Shad Helmstetter, PhD, *What to Say When You Talk to Yourself*, Pocket, 1982.
- John G. Watkins and Helen H. Watkins, *Ego States: Theory and Therapy*, W. W. Norton, 1997.

41

Repeat Yourself

Just as interrupting yourself (seemingly an excursion into paralysis) actually invites you into a liberating self-awareness, repeating yourself (seemingly an excursion into bland uniformity) is actually an exercise in endless variation. As you'll discover in this exercise, the harder you try to execute precise repetition, the more variety you will uncover.

What You'll Need
- Your voice
- A sentence

How to Do It
1. **Choose a sentence.** Make it a good one, something that feels rich and complex when you say it out loud. Consider using the opening sentence of a favorite book (see page 221 for one idea) or even writing one of your own.

2. **Memorize the sentence.** For purposes of immersion, no reading is allowed.

3. **Say it out loud.** Speak just once at first, slowly and purposefully. Let the sound of the words fill the room. As you speak, also try to be the audience for the sound of your own voice. This can be difficult. Try to hear all the nuances: the rhythm of the phrasing, the tone of the words. But also hear *yourself*: the quality of your own voice and your performance. Where do you pause? Where do you stumble? Where do you get it just right?

4. **Memorize your performance.** Stay silent for a moment and try to hear a precise echo of your voice, mistakes and all. Mentally rehearse speaking the sentence in exactly the same way you just did.

5. **Repeat yourself.** Now say it out loud again. Try to resist the impulse to correct mistakes or to improve on your performance. Imagine that you are a tape recorder. It's an impossible task, of course, so just notice the changes that happen despite your efforts at precision. At the same time, try to hold in mind the original version. Continue repeating, pausing between each repetition to review the accuracy of the reproduction and to bring back to mind the original performance. Stop when you can repeat it perfectly or when your head is spinning, whichever comes first.

The Best Sentence Ever Written

For my money, it's the opening sentence in Gabriel García Márquez's *One Hundred Years of Solitude*: "Many years later, as he faced the firing squad, Colonel Aureliano Buendía was to remember that distant afternoon when his father took him to discover ice."

Variations: More of the Same

Record yourself. In this variation, you record your actual voice using a recorder. The complication, of course, is that how your voice sounds when played back to you is different than the way it sounds in your own head. As a result, the experience is as much like imitating someone else as it is like repeating yourself. To complicate matters further, you can try repeating yourself along with the recording.

Practice mimicry. I have a good ear for music and sound, but I am hopeless as a mimic. Any time I try to put on any sort of accent, I inevitably sound like Apu on *The Simpsons*. Surely you can do better than I can. Choose a well-known person who has a distinctive accent (ex-presidents are a good option here) and try doing this exercise mimicking that voice as you speak the sentence.

Ask how you get to Carnegie Hall. If you are a musician, you do a variation of this exercise whenever you practice, especially when you practice scales, arpeggios, and other such exercises. In this case, however, you

are trying *not* to imitate your mistakes. You can try it by taking a simple phrase and imagining the sound of a perfect performance of those notes. Then try to re-create that performance on your own. This variation works with other art forms as well. Picture in your mind the hands of God and Adam on the ceiling of the Sistine Chapel. Try to draw them. Then try again. And again. What evolves with each repetition?

Minimalize. The minimalist movement in classical music is a great illustration of the ideas underlying this exercise. In the music of composers like Steve Reich and Philip Glass, the classical ideal of "theme and variation" is transformed: a theme, endlessly repeated, reveals endless variation in the perception of the listener. Try doing this exercise in the role of the audience rather than the performer, listening to one of the pieces listed in the next section and trying to hear the intersection between repetition and variation.

Further Listening: Minimalist Masterpieces
- Philip Glass, *Music in Twelve Parts*, Nonesuch (79324), 1993.
- Alvin Lucier, *I Am Sitting in a Room*, Lovely Music (LCD 1013), 1993.
- Steve Reich, *Music for 18 Musicians*, ECM (1129), 2000.
- Terry Riley, *In C*, Sony Classical (88697453682), 2009.

Retrace Your Steps

42

Who said that life can only move in one direction? Spend a few minutes tracking backward through your actions and discover what your life feels like when it's lived in reverse.

What You'll Need
- Your memory
- Paper and a pen

How to Do It
1. **Get present.** Before you move into the past, take a moment to ground yourself solidly in the present moment. Sit comfortably, look around, and orient yourself to each of your senses.
2. **Start the list.** Think about the last hour of your life, and then write down the major events that took place during that time, in reverse order. Let's say you made a phone call, went to the bathroom, drove the kids to

school, and cleaned up the dishes. Write each of these down, leaving plenty of space between each entry.

3. **Fill in the details.** Now focus on the first item on your list. Staying in reverse order, fill in the sequence of steps that composed that event. So for the phone call, your list might look something like this: *I hung up the phone; I told my friend that I had to get going; I told my friend that I'd be happy to loan her the book she was interested in; I listened to my friend as she asked about a book I'd recently read; I told my friend that I was getting over a cold; my friend asked me how I was doing; I picked up the phone; the phone rang.* More details will undoubtedly emerge as you write. Feel free to fill them in where they belong. You'll be tempted to cheat by remembering the sequence of events in forward order and just writing them down in reverse. Try to resist this temptation.

4. **Run the film backward.** Looking at your completed list, can you mentally reexperience in reverse the past few moments of your life with a flowing motion? Visualize it like a film that's running backward. Don't worry if you struggle here, but be as persistent as you can.

5. **Forward, march!** When you feel like you can't stand it any longer, release yourself from the mental effort that backward movement requires and flush out the memory by starting at the beginning and remembering it all in forward motion.

Do Geese See God?

Forward motion is a powerful cognitive reflex. And our reflexes are exceptionally difficult to override. As a result, even though the narrative of our lives is heavily shaped by our memories of the past, even though we are constantly going backward into memory in order to understand our experience, we still replay our memories only in forward motion. It's nearly impossible to do otherwise. That's why watching filmed images in reverse never ceases to be hypnotic; suddenly we're able to see something that our minds usually refuse to let us experience. It's also why thinking about palindromes can feel so maddening; they defy the ordinary cognitive structures of our minds. Doing this exercise is like trying to live life without using your dominant hand. It's not impossible, but you have to work so hard to overcome your own reflexes that everything becomes slower and more awkward. Your life becomes more deliberate, and more conscious.

Variations: Further Adventures in Backtracking

Act it out. As challenging as it can be to mentally reverse your movement, physically reenacting your behavior backward takes it up another notch. Start with a very small series of motions—just a few seconds of physical movement—and try to re-create it in reverse. Watch the many ways in which your reflexes get in your way.

Blink, sneeze, hiccup. Since your reflexes are at issue, take some time to observe your body's reflexive behavior as it moves through the world. How much of what you do is intentional and how much is involuntary? How much control can you exercise over the movements and behaviors that occur reflexively?

Become a reverse engineer. Engineers and computer programmers have made careers out of reverse engineering other people's products. Take a manufactured item from your life and try to mentally reconstruct its invention, starting from the finished product.

Get palindromic. Just reading a palindrome is a pretty good mental workout. But if you really want to get your mind working in two directions at once, try creating one. Pick a word with potential (*banana*, say) and start working out in both directions.

Further Reading: Books on Palindromes and Hindsight

- Howard W. Bergerson, *Palindromes and Anagrams*, Dover Publications, 1973.
- Michael Donner, *I Love Me, Vol. 1: S. Wordrow's Palindrome Encyclopedia*, Algonquin Books, 1996.
- Mark Freeman, *Hindsight: The Promise and Peril of Looking Backward*, Oxford University Press, 2010.

Hear White Noise

All sound is music; we're just not used to hearing it that way. People with perfect pitch can identify the tones in sounds we don't think of as tonal—the hum of the refrigerator, the whir of a fan. Even if we are unable to identify the notes, these sounds are performing a subtle orchestral performance around us all the time. Take a moment to hear the secret symphony taking place wherever you are.

What You'll Need

- A reasonably quiet room

How to Do It

1. **Choose a room.** It can be a room with or without appliances in it. A kitchen will work fine, but so will a basement. (Don't worry about it being too quiet. Absolute silence is exceptionally rare.) This is a good exercise to do in a room that you spend a lot of time

in; you may notice subtle sonic influences that you'll want to change.

2. **Eliminate any identifiably pitched or percussive sounds.** Turn off the radio or television if either's on. But also notice other, subtler sounds, like ticking clocks or a pacing dog. Try to remove the source of as many of these sounds as you can.

3. **Quiet yourself. Remember that you are also a source of sound.** Before you begin to focus on the sounds around you, take a moment to notice the sounds that you yourself are creating, and to quiet them as much as possible. Are you tapping your fingers without realizing it? Are you breathing audibly? What noise does your clothing make when your body moves? How about skin against skin? Breathe slowly, quiet your movements, and settle in.

4. **Start listening.** The first sound or two will probably come quickly and easily. In fact, you probably noticed them even before you got to this step. The whir of a computer's fan. The hum of the refrigerator. The low rumble of the furnace. Try to hold each of these sounds in mind and, at the same time, to listen deeper. There's more there, I promise. Some of these sounds will be constant. Others will come and go periodically. Maybe it's the faint sound of the wind outside or of traffic from a distant highway. Place each sound spa-

tially. If you're a visually oriented person, you might think of these sounds as layers of color in a watercolor painting. Each can be distinctly observed, but at the same time, the line between each sound blurs at the point of contact.

5. **Hear the music.** Now listen deeper to all the different sounds that you have identified. Try to hear the pitch, or pitches, within each one. You don't have to be particularly musical to do this. Just try to hum at the same pitch as the sound you are listening to. Notice how the different tones shift in time. Notice the rhythms within each source of sound and then between each of them. Notice whether the different pitches seem harmonious or whether they seem to clash. Imagine for a moment that these sounds have been deliberately chosen to create a particular musical effect. Finally, give a title to the composition.

What Color Is That Noise?

Semi-technically speaking, white noise is defined as a combination of all tonal frequencies into a single sound. It's a term that's borrowed from the concept of white light, which is light that's made up of a combination of all the possible different colors. You can get more technical, if you want ... a *lot* more technical. But really, you know white noise when you hear it. It's the sound of an analog

television set tuned to no station, the ocean from a distance, or all the air-conditioning units in Manhattan on a hot summer day.

The funny thing is, none of these are *actually* white noise, because white noise is in fact just a theoretical concept. As a matter of fact, they might be brown, pink, or gray noise (all of which are mathematical formulas describing the different distribution of sonic frequencies within a single sound). In fact, this exercise works precisely because the noise *isn't* white, because you can hear and isolate specific frequencies within the sounds around you.

Variations: Listening Deeper

Go outside. Ambient sound is different outside than it is inside. I first tried this exercise early one morning in college. I had just finished doing a middle-of-the-night radio program, and when I went outside at seven o'clock, the campus was quiet and empty. I'm not even sure why, but I sat down on the grass and just started listening to every sound I could hear, forcing myself to go deeper and deeper into the softest distant murmurs. The more I listened, the more I could hear.

Pay attention to soundtracks. As this exercise may have made you aware, the sounds in your environment can have a powerful effect on your state of mind. We all know, for instance, that the music used in movies and television programs powerfully enhances our emotional experience of watching those shows. But it is quite difficult to simultaneously watch a show and remain aware of the effect of its soundtrack. The next time you're watching a movie, try to force yourself into awareness of the soundtrack and its effect on your experience. Notice how quickly this focus slips away.

Explore emotional soundtracks. This is a concept I owe to some of my postgraduate trainers who talked about the metaphorical soundtracks that play inside our own heads at different moments in our lives. In particular, they described how people who have survived trauma seem to hear something like the theme song from *Jaws* when they are confronted with something that reminds them of the original trauma. The next time you have a distinctly amplified emotional experience—positive *or* negative—take a moment to try to describe the secret soundtrack that is playing in the back of your mind. Then imagine what the experience would be with different music playing, or with no music at all.

Consider psychoacoustics. It's not just *what* we hear; it's *how* we hear. And the way we hear is powerfully influenced by the way our brain processes sound. It's not something you can easily make yourself aware of, but knowing the ways in which your mind is influencing sound will make you listen differently to the sounds around you.

Further Reading: Books on the Music of Sound

- Jean-François Augoyard and Henry Torgue, eds., *Sonic Experience: A Guide to Everyday Sounds*, McGill-Queen's University Press, 2006.
- Perry R. Cook, ed., *Music, Cognition, and Computerized Sound: An Introduction to Psychoacoustics*, MIT Press, 1999.
- David Huron, *Sweet Anticipation: Music and the Psychology of Expectation,* MIT Press, 2006.
- Robert Jourdain, *Music, the Brain, and Ecstasy: How Music Captures Our Imagination*, Quill, 2002.
- Joshua Leeds, T*he Power of Sound: How to Manage Your Personal Soundscape for a Vital, Productive, and Healthy Life*, Healing Arts Press, 2001.
- Daniel J. Levitin, *This Is Your Brain on Music: The Science of a Human Obsession*, Dutton, 2006.

44

Dig in Your Heels

This is a variation on the technique of progressive relaxation, in which you release the tension in your body by first clenching different muscles as tightly as possible. The idea is paradoxical but simple: in order to feel relaxation, you first have to become aware of the contrasting tension you are often holding unconsciously. It's an idea that can work just as effectively in the psychological realm. Here you will use it to sharpen your sense of motivation, by identifying a goal and then refusing to do it.

What You'll Need
- A near-term, achievable goal
- A heavy chair that won't move easily when you push against it

How to Do It
1. **Choose a goal.** The best type of goal for this exercise will have a quality of active tension when you think

about it. Consider things that you know are good for you, like doing a daily meditation practice or getting your cholesterol checked. It might be something that you feel guilty about not having done already. It should be something that you know you could achieve fairly easily if only you would take a few simple steps.

2. **Get comfortable.** To begin the exercise, try to achieve a sense of stasis. The chair that you've chosen for the exercise should be heavy and immobile, and, ideally, extremely comfortable. Sit in it and try to get yourself into a state in which you have absolutely no desire to move.

3. **Assume the position.** With your hands by your side, extend your legs slightly and raise your toes so that only your heels are in contact with the floor. Imagine yourself as the anchor in a game of tug-of-war. Don't apply pressure, yet; just feel the potential for resistance. Inhale slowly. Exhale.

4. **Resist.** Now close your eyes and imagine the tug-of-war rope tied around your waist. On the other end of that rope are all the reasons you should move forward and accomplish the goal you identified in step 1. Those reasons are starting to tug at you, gently at first but growing steadily stronger. Say, "I won't." Keep repeating this phrase as you brace yourself in your chair and push

against the floor with your heels. Keep holding in this position. At some point, you'll start to have a powerful urge to relax your muscles and let go. Don't do it yet. Instead, pull back a little harder. Soon you'll start to feel like you simply *can't* maintain the tension any more. But you can hold it just a little longer. Play it all the way out, the way you would an actual, fiercely fought game of tug-of-war, until your body truly loses the ability to continue resisting.

5. **Give in.** When your body gives in, don't just relax. Close your eyes and imagine yourself being pulled forward, irresistibly, by the rope. You're flying forward. Immerse yourself in this sensation and let it evolve, from that first rough jerk to a sense of sailing effortlessly. Let your muscles relax; let all the resistance flow out of you. When you feel yourself coming to a stop, take one last slow breath and then open your eyes. As you move back into your day, let the energy of the exercise carry you forward.

Prescribing the Symptom

I know I'm going to get in trouble for this, but I'm going to do it anyway. I'm going to give away a secret therapist trick. In fact, I'm about to give away one of the most important secrets behind this entire book. So be forewarned. If you read the rest of this section, you might not

need this book (or your therapist) anymore. You might be able to do it all on your own.

It's called *paradoxical intervention*, or "prescribing the symptom."

That's a fancy way of saying that you get put into a double bind. Here's an example: Say you go to a therapist for help in managing your fear of speaking in public. You describe to the doctor how you get paralyzed with anxiety whenever you have to talk in front of groups. You just can't seem to get it under control. At the end of the session, the therapist tells you that it's very important for the treatment that over the next week you *continue* to feel your fear of speaking in public. In fact, you should try to worry about it even more, to intensify your fear.

You leave the session in a state of confusion, wondering if your therapist is completely out of her mind. But whether or not she is sane, you still have to figure out what to do next. If you follow her instructions, you can't help but acknowledge that you have control over how you experience your symptoms, and thus that you have the ability to improve them. On the other hand, the only way to *not* follow her instructions is to worry less. This is the bind. So even if you do nothing, you have already altered your state of mind. You shift from being the person who is afraid to being the person observing the fear. Either way, something has changed.

Variations: Put Yourself in Paradoxical Positions

Prescribe your own symptoms. Make a list of your own "symptoms," whatever they happen to be, however you'd like to define them. Think about parts of your own behavior that you feel unable to control—worries, negative thoughts, and so on. Then see if you can put yourself in a bind by instructing yourself to do more of the same.

Enact other clichés. There are many postural clichés that we use to describe our lives: "Put your foot down," "Get all bent out of shape," "Get your arms around something." Choose one and discover the truth beneath the cliché by enacting it physically.

Further Reading: Books on Paradox

- Jerry Fletcher and Kelle Olwyler, *Paradoxical Thinking: How to Profit from Your Contradictions*, Berrett-Koehler Publishers, 1997.
- Mardy Grothe, *Oxymoronica: Paradoxical Wit and Wisdom from History's Greatest Wordsmiths*, HarperCollins, 2004.
- Gary Hayden and Michael Picard, *This Book Does Not Exist: Adventures in the Paradoxical*, Fall River Press, 2009.
- Andreas Wagner, *Paradoxical Life: Meaning, Matter, and the Power of Human Choice*, Yale University Press, 2009.

45

Pout

"**M**om always liked *you* best."

We laugh whenever we hear someone say it, but it's a bittersweet laugh because we know that no matter how old we grow, there will always be childhood hurts that we continue to feel as if they had only just happened. Sure, we've learned to put them aside and act "mature." But we haven't forgotten. Take a few minutes to release your inner pouty child and set him/her free to stomp and fume and dissipate some of that old resentment.

What You'll Need
- The memory of a childhood injustice
- Your lips

How to Do It
1. **Identify a moment of injustice from your childhood.** Make it simple and primitive. (Sibling rivalry is usually a good source of material here.) The ideal

injustice will be one you can feel with the original child-hood energy while your adult self can find humor in it.

2. **Now put it out of your mind.** You know how to do this. You've been doing it your whole life. Can't you just hear the adults around you, telling you to stop dwelling on it, move on, and get over it?

3. **Stick out your lips.** Try to start your pout without emotion, simply by assuming the correct posture. And the key element in any good pout is a good set of pro-truding lips. As you push your lips outward, hunch your shoulders, crane your neck upward, raise your eyebrows pleadingly, and direct your eyes toward the ceiling. Imagine that you are pushing your entire face away from your skull. If you're doing it right, your lips should start to quiver. Feel free to let the rest of your body tighten up into a near spasm. Hold this position as best you can through the last two steps.

4. **Bring on the emotion.** Your posture should have already begun to induce a state of partial poutiness, even in the absence of relevant emotions. Now bring back the specific memory you identified in step 1. Imagine that you are pleading with an adult to address the injustice. Let the emotions and the posture merge into one big self-reinforcing state of misery.

5. **Imagine an alternative ending.** You *know* how this went the first time around. What would have worked

better? Acknowledging both the truth of your sense of injustice and the reality that we can't always get what we want, try to imagine a way through this impasse that would have prevented it from becoming a lifelong source of resentment. As you do this (and don't worry if you can't figure it all out right now), let your face and body relax and take a few slow breaths as you allow yourself to return to a full awareness of your adult self. Give your whole body a good shake, and then continue on about your business.

You'd Better Not Pout

As this exercise should make clear, pouting makes use of emotion, but it isn't really *about* emotion. Pouting is an *interpersonal* power play. Think about it: aside from doing this exercise, you would never truly pout when you're alone. Pouts are made for public consumption. The posture is one of utter weakness and helplessness, like that of a submissive puppy. But there is a demand behind it, and usually anger as well. Pouting says, "Because I am powerless, you have to do what I ask."

This is why pouting aggravates parents so much. When children pout, parents feel manipulated. So most parents do everything in their power to extinguish the behavior.

But "manipulation" is a tricky issue. It's often inappropriately attributed to children's behavior. When I work with parents who say they are feeling "manipulated" by their children, I always redefine that word: *manipulation* is what children do to try to get their needs met when they are unable, for whatever reason, to ask for something directly. The question I try to help parents ask is, "What is my child needing right now, and what is keeping him or her from asking for it directly?"

The relevant point of this exercise is that somewhere, buried deep down in the pouty memory you identified at the beginning, is a genuine need that went unmet. It's underneath everything, even the emotions. Can you identify that need and express it in the sort of simple words that you would have used at the time, had you been able?

Variations: Other Ways to Liberate Your Angry Inner Child

Sulk. This is a close cousin to pouting that uses more sophisticated strategies. Pouting is basically a short-term activity (it's hard to maintain that pose for long), but a good sulk can go on for days. Sulking can't be reduced to a single posture; it's more of an attitude.

Stomp your feet. This one is all about using big sounds as a way to disguise your inherent feeling of small-ness. It's like a tiny frog that can make monstrously loud noises to scare off predators. We almost never truly stomp

our feet as adults, but maybe we should; it feels really good, and it's highly likely to end in laughter.

Throw a tantrum. This should obviously be done with care. As with pouting and the other activities listed here, a true childish tantrum is done solely for the benefit of others, so doing it alone will feel a little funny. I recommend the classic technique of throwing yourself on a bed and pounding it with your fists while kicking with your feet. Start by enacting the behavior without any particular emotional content. Then when you feel ready, you can try it again, using a childhood memory like the one you identified for this exercise.

Further Reading: Working with Negative and Destructive Emotions

- Antonio R. Damasio, *The Feeling of What Happens: Body and Emotion in the Making of Consciousness*, Harvest Books, 1999.

- Daniel Goleman, *Destructive Emotions: How Can We Overcome Them?: A Scientific Dialogue with the Dalai Lama*, Bantam, 2004.

- Daniel Goleman, ed., *Healing Emotions: Conversations with the Dalai Lama on Mindfulness, Emotions, and Health*, Shambhala, 1997.

- Joseph LeDoux, *The Emotional Brain: The Mysterious Underpinnings of Emotional Life*, Simon & Schuster, 1996.

46

Speak

Speech is an exhalation of breath, given shape by the posture and movement of your body. You emerged from the womb knowing how to make sounds. But learning to shape those sounds into language took several years. Start again from the beginning and let yourself rediscover the anatomical gymnastics that take place behind the scenes during even the simplest conversations.

What You'll Need
- Your breath
- Your vocal chords
- Your mouth

How to Do It
1. **Groan.** Start with the basics. Let your mouth sag open, take a deep breath, and then push out the air, making a groaning sound. Let the sound settle at whatever pitch it naturally finds. Try to keep your mouth

and tongue (and the rest of your body) still. Just hear and feel the undifferentiated sound. As you do this, see if you can ease your mind out of its adult awareness a little. Make noise the way an infant does. Try to surrender to the unformed feeling of the sound that you are making.

2. **Start shaping the sound.** Now, continuing to make a groaning sound with each exhalation, open your mouth as wide as you can. Hear how the sound changes as you do this. Slowly close your mouth until the "aaaaahhh" sound becomes a "hhhmmmm." Listen to the shifting sound as you continue to slowly open and close your mouth. If you listen carefully, you should be able to hear the "overtones" created by your voice, a slight, high-pitched whistlelike sound that changes in pitch as you open and close your mouth.

3. **Introduce vowels.** Now start introducing some familiar vocal postures. Do this first without making any accompanying sound. Simply shape your mouth into the position it needs to be in to make each vowel sound. Feel how naturally and easily your mouth moves into each position, the way a violinist's fingers just "know" where each note is on an unmarked fret. Hold in each position for a moment and notice how many of your facial muscles have to work together to pull it off. Now, bring sound back in. Make each vowel

sound separately; then try moving continuously through the vowel sequence. Consider the fact that the positions that mark English vowels are entirely arbitrary. Each point between each vowel could be defined as a meaningful unit.

4. **Add consonants.** This is where things can begin to get really complex. Making vowel sounds requires us to hold our mouth in a static position. Creating consonants requires control over both our breath and a range of micromovements involving our lips, tongue, and teeth. But since we're just learning to speak here, let's keep it simple and start with two consonants, both of which involve your lips: *m* and *p*. First, just place your lips in the starting position for each sound. Then make the movement for each letter without adding any breath. (You'll notice that *m* is essentially silent, while *p* contains the sound made by a small puff of air being expelled from your mouth.) Finally, make the sounds out loud. If you're feeling ambitious here, you can work your way through the alphabet the same way you did in step 3, noticing both the muscular coordination required for each sound and how many other sounds your mouth has the potential to make.

5. **Your first word.** No matter what your parents have told you, I'm willing to bet that your *actual* first word was "mama." Honestly, what at eighteen months could

you possibly have been more motivated to say? So, using the techniques you've been practicing in the first four steps, slowly form that word, feeling the full complexity of your body as it coordinates your breath, tone, and facial musculature into the simple miracle of a spoken word. Finally, as you move back into your regular life, see if you can maintain your awareness of how much expertise you are demonstrating each time you use your voice to speak.

What We Don't Know

When you listen carefully to a language you don't understand, you can really hear how limited a portion of the possible range of human vocalization we actually use in whatever language we happen to speak. As this exercise should make clear, there are many sounds that we are able to make that we never do simply because we have not defined them as elements of speech in our native tongue. Our categories for what is and is not an identifiable linguistic sound are developed in early infancy. This is true not only for sounds we're able to produce but also for sounds we're able to recognize. In fact, it can be true even within our own language. I learned this the hard way when I discovered during my freshman year of college that I can't recognize the distinction between the vowel sound in the words *awed* and *odd*. (The parent to whom I was speaking didn't appreciate my describing her child, who had just been awed by something I'd just done, as "odd.") To me, they are simply the same sound. I don't know why I can't hear or imitate that distinction—I've often tried. But that is precisely the point. It's not simply that I didn't know the difference between those two sounds; I didn't even know that I didn't know.

Variations: Further Forays into Human Speech

Try to speak while inhaling. This simple variation that is impossible to do.

Whisper. If you tried the "speak while inhaling" variation, you probably wound up compromising at a whisper. Whispering is speech without tone (that is, without the vocal chords vibrating). Spend some time limiting your speech to a whisper. How does doing this affect your state of mind?

E-nun-ci-ate. You know, "The rain in Spain stays mainly in the plain." Enunciation and diction exercises have mostly gone out of style. Whether that's a good thing or not is open to debate, but the act of speaking extremely clearly is not only useful for making yourself understood. By exaggerating the physical aspects of speech, you can more easily feel the incredible mechanical logistics that make speaking possible.

Further Reading: Books on Speech

- Dr. Morton Cooper, *Change Your Voice, Change Your Life: A Quick, Simple Plan for Finding and Using Your Natural Dynamic Voice*, Wilshire Book Co., 1996.
- Jeffrey C. Hahner, Martin A. Sokoloff, and Sandra L. Salisch, *Speaking Clearly: Improving Voice and Diction*, McGraw-Hill, 2002.
- Janet Rodgers, *The Complete Voice and Speech Workout: 74 Exercises for Classroom and Studio Use*, Applause Books, 2002.
- J. Anthony Seikel, Douglas W. King, and David G. Drumright, *Anatomy and Physiology for Speech, Language, and Hearing*, 4th Edition, Delmar Cengage Learning, 2010.

47

Dwell in the Past

People tell you not to do it. The past is gone; move on. But what are our true selves constructed of if not of our past experiences? Grant yourself permission to hang out in the past for a few minutes, to dwell there.

What You'll Need
- The memory of a difficult act of self-transformation

How to Do It
1. **Choose a point in the past to dwell on.** Start by making a quick mental list of the biggest, hardest changes that you have made in your life—the sorts of changes that you needed to make in order to survive and that make you who you are today, like giving up an addiction or leaving an abusive relationship. Current problems and crises are likely to come to mind, but for the purpose of this exercise, choose something that feels pretty solidly resolved.

2. **Feel yourself fully in the present.** Before you begin to dwell in the past, develop a clear point of contrast. Take a moment to look around at your current environment. Anchor this awareness in all your senses; try saying out loud what you see and where you are, what you smell and hear and feel. Breathe in and feel your body, scanning downward from the top of your head and through your arms and chest, your pelvis, legs, and feet. Feel your feet solidly in contact with the ground. Say your name out loud.

3. **Re-create the hard place from the past.** Bring back to mind the personal change that you identified in step 1. Starting from that point of change, move backward in time to a point just before the transformation happened. Isolate a single physical place that feels most emblematic of your state prior to the transformation. Close your eyes and try to re-create the physical space in which the hard change occurred. Just as you did in step 2, make it all vividly real. Describe the place out loud, moving through each of your senses. It's possible that you'll notice yourself resisting the memory, not wanting to go back. That's okay. Just notice it. Tell yourself that you're safe. You're dwelling in this moment, but you can leave whenever you please.

4. **Locate the seeds of change.** Now shift the perspective and try to see the same scene as if you were

watching yourself on a movie screen. What does your past self look like? Perhaps no one could have looked at you at that moment and predicted the transformation you were about to undergo. But the seeds of change were there, and in the present you are in a perfect position to look back in time and see them. Study yourself and try to identify what was happening inside you that made the difference. Be sure to give yourself full credit here. "I'd just hit rock bottom" won't cut it. There was something in you at that time that was ready to change. What was it?

5. **Return to the present.** Open your eyes and repeat the instructions for step 2, anchoring yourself to the present again. Even as you do this, feel how the traces of your past dwellings linger over the present. Don't try to push them away. Just ask yourself, "What do I want to carry forward with me? What do I want to leave behind?"

Dwelling

It's both a noun and a verb. It holds both spatial and temporal meanings. It has taken on a negative connotation of immobility and paralysis, and at the same time it is a word, like *home*, that evokes powerful positive associations. What is this strange split in our psyche, this ambivalence about residence?

The word itself embodies the tension between our awareness of perpetual change and our desire to have something solid and unchangeable to hold on to as we move through the world. It is a beautiful word in just this way, balancing yin and yang, reminding us that it is always possible to find movement within stillness, and stillness within movement.

Variations: Movement within Stillness

Dwell in the future. We all sometimes imagine who and where we will be in the future. Try a variation on this exercise in which you start with a change you would *like* to make in your life, and then picture your future self in the physical space you will inhabit once you have made that change.

Refuse to dwell. If life is constant change, experiment with trying to live it as such. Notice all the apparent stillness in your life in the present moment. What would it mean to put that stillness into motion?

Further Reading: Books on Dwelling Places

- Winifred Gallagher, *House Thinking: A Room-by-Room Look at How We Live*, HarperCollins, 2006.
- Linda Hogan, *Dwellings: A Spiritual History of the Living World*, Touchstone, 2006.

- Mary Beth Lagerborg, *Dwelling: Living Fully from the Space You Call Home*, Revell, 2007.
- Clare Cooper Marcus, *House as a Mirror of Self: Exploring the Deeper Meaning of Home*, Conari Press, 1997.
- Witold Rybczynski, *Home: A Short History of an Idea*, Penguin Books, 1987.

48

Stand Up

We take gravity for granted, but it's always there, keeping us from floating away. Take a few minutes to heighten your awareness of gravity, imagining that it has grown so strong that it is pinning you down to the ground, making the simple act of standing up a great accomplishment.

What You'll Need
- A soft floor
- A chair to lift yourself up on

How to Do It
1. **Lie down.** Lie on your back next to the chair in a splayed position, with your arms and legs tossed out to your sides. Take a moment while you're in this position to check in with your body. Breathe normally as you mentally scan through different muscle groups. Notice any tension you find. Take a moment to close your eyes and relax.

2. **Tune in to gravity.** As your body starts to relax, let a sensation of heaviness come over you. Feel the line of contact between your body and the floor. Each time you exhale, imagine that the floor is pulling you closer to it. Let your body become magnetized to the floor. Imagine that you are losing muscle tone, that even your bones are softening. You are turning into an amoeba, losing the ability to control your own movement.

3. **Resist gravity.** You should be starting to feel something akin to sleep paralysis, that strange sensation you sometimes have when you wake up but don't yet have control over your voluntary muscles. Feeling this detachment from your body, raise both your arms an inch or two above the floor, keeping your muscles as relaxed as possible. Hold them like that for as long as you can. When you can't maintain the position any longer, let them fall back to the floor. Do the same thing with your legs. Feel how powerfully gravity is pulling them downward.

4. **Stand.** Slide your hands down to your sides. Then, bracing yourself with your elbows, push yourself into a sitting position. As you do this, try holding on to the sensation of lost muscle strength. Then, place your arms on the seat of the chair and slowly lift yourself into a stand. Feel the pull of the earth against you. Let yourself lean, tip, and wobble.

5. Release. Focus deeply on this sensation: the delicate balance between the pull of the earth beneath you and your capacity to keep your balance while standing upright. Feel how the mere act of standing requires the continuous use of your muscles. Gravity is always working against you, always trying to pull you back to the floor. As you move through your day, you will, of course, need to let go of this level of awareness of gravity, but try to let an echo of it remain with you, reminding you that your upright self exists in a delicate balance with larger, unseen forces.

Acts of Faith

Do you believe in gravity?

It sounds like an absurd question. But gravity, like so many other principles that we use to guide and regulate our lives, is simply a concept developed to explain what we observe in the world. Yes, its existence can easily be demonstrated—just toss something in the air. But there could conceivably be other explanations. After all, there was a time when it was impossible to imagine that the earth was not the center of the solar system. And as the continuing debate over climate change shows, even when ideas can be clearly scientifically demonstrated, individuals still have the choice to believe or not. Do you believe that the earth is round? Do you believe in the unconscious?

Do you believe in global warming? Do you believe in God? Belief is a complex act, a choice and a commitment. And in the end, on some level, it's simply an act of faith.

Variations: More Ways to Defy Gravity

Jump. It's fun. But be careful because it makes gravity angry. Stand in place with your legs apart at shoulder length. Bend into a squat. Then push your body as far into the air as you can. You'll be back down on the ground in no time. Much too quickly, in fact, to be able to fully take in everything that is happening during your brief rise and fall. Do it again, trying to focus your attention on the force that you are resisting. Can you isolate the moment when rising turns into falling?

Improve your posture. I've been talking about standing up as if it's a single, unified thing. But, of course, there are many ways to stand. And as long as you're already standing, why not take the opportunity to improve your posture? See the books listed in the next section for a few ideas on how to do this.

Use magnetism. Or as I like to call it, sideways gravity. There are several ways of going about incorporating magnetism into this exercise. One is to repeat the exercise using the wall instead of the floor (this obviously increases the level of difficulty because the forces of attraction are imaginary rather than actual). Another is to do the exercise

as if your own *body* possessed a massive gravitational pull. How does the world look when *you* are the center of gravity?

Further Reading: Books on Gravity and Posture

- Mary Bond, *The New Rules of Posture: How to Sit, Stand, and Move in the Modern World*, Healing Arts Press, 2006.
- David Darling, *Gravity's Arc: The Story of Gravity, from Aristotle to Einstein and Beyond*, Wiley, 2006.
- John W. Moffat, *Reinventing Gravity: A Physicist Goes Beyond Einstein*, Smithsonian Books/Collins, 2008.
- Bernard Schutz, *Gravity from the Ground Up: An Introductory Guide to Gravity and General Relativity*, Cambridge University Press, 2003.
- Missy Vineyard, *How You Stand, How You Move, How You Live: Learning the Alexander Technique to Explore Your Mind-Body Connection and Achieve Self-Mastery*, Marlow & Company, 2007.

49

Accept Reality

Because, really, what other choice is there for you? Everything is exactly as it is in this, the present moment. Our desire to change things—about ourselves, about others, about the world—doesn't change *that*. Reality is a good thing. Take a few minutes to practice being *in* reality, in one small way.

What You'll Need
- A character flaw
- A pen and paper

How to Do It
1. **Choose a flaw.** Your biggest deficits might come to mind right away. But for the purposes of this exercise, it's important to think small. Isolate a small, mildly embarrassing behavior, something you don't like to acknowledge to others. It could be something as simple as the fact that you secretly drink milk straight from the

carton. Write it down, as simply and directly as possible: "I secretly drink milk from the carton."

2. **Breathe.** Sit quietly for a few moments. Check in with your body. Take a deep, slow breath. Exhale. At the bottom of the exhalation, say to yourself, "I accept." For now, don't focus on your flaw or on anything in particular. Just let a general feeling of acceptance gather around you.

3. **Focus on the flaw.** Now bring the chosen flaw back into your mind. Continuing to breathe calmly and deeply, try to notice the emotions, thoughts, and physical sensations that arise when you think about the flaw. Do certain muscles reflexively tighten? Does a sense of shame arise? What do you think about yourself when you think about this flaw? Let all these things arise without censorship. They are the parts of you that conspire to keep you out of reality. See if you can maintain an awareness of both the flaw and the parts of you that can't tolerate its existence.

4. **Magnify the flaw.** Here's the hardest part: Rather than letting go of the flaw, try to make it bigger in your mind. Make it so big that it becomes absurd. So if your flaw is that you secretly drink milk from the carton, imagine that this behavior is an obsession, it's all you ever think about. Imagine that it is causing other people terrible harm. Now try to describe the behavior in the broadest

and most global way possible. For instance, you might say, "I am a devious, secretive liar who contaminates the people around me." Check in with your emotions. If you're feeling any true shame or embarrassment, you haven't magnified the flaw enough yet. You'll know that you're getting it right when the statement feels so absurd that you can't say it without smiling. Write down that statement, below the unmagnified statement you wrote in step 1.

5. **Accept.** Repeat the breathing exercise in step 2, again without focusing on anything in particular. When you are ready, look back at the statement you wrote down in step 1. Say to yourself, "I accept that ..." Complete the sentence with the statement you wrote down. How true does it feel when you say it? If it doesn't feel completely true, don't worry about it; just notice that a part of you is stubbornly refusing to be in reality. Ask yourself what it would take to make the statement feel true. Take another deep breath and then continue on with your day.

Working with Resistance

This simple exercise can be difficult for people in many different ways. Many people struggle because their sense of shame is so powerful that it doesn't allow them to settle into a mood of acceptance. (If you found that to be the case, try doing it again with an even more insignificant flaw. Or even try doing it using an *invented* character flaw.) For those with a strong sense of justice, the idea of acceptance can feel like failure because it gets tangled up with the idea of inaction. For me (and I'm sure for many others as well), the difficulty arises because the idea of *accepting* something has become entwined with the idea of *surrendering* to someone. I find that there is no easy resolution to this dilemma. I have to prove to myself, again and again, that this is not the case. Each time I overcome my resistance and allow myself to experience a full awareness of how things are in the present moment, I rediscover the profound truth that acceptance is not the same as enslavement. In fact, the experience of deep acceptance is truly liberating and empowering.

Variations: More Paths Toward Acceptance

Confess. The early Catholics knew what they were doing when they invented the confessional. As this exercise should have demonstrated, we expend an awful lot of energy behind the scenes trying to keep ourselves from being too aware of our flaws. Confession allows us to release that energy by speaking the truth. But for it to work, the person or institution to whom we are confessing has to feel unthreatening, or anonymous. Select an audience that is both of those things to you (a pet is an excellent choice) and unburden yourtself. It's not exactly a religious experience, but it might be even better.

Catch yourself looking unattractive. You know that you don't always look your best, and if you're like most people, you wince when you get a glimpse of your less-flattering physical self in the mirror or in a photograph. Next time this happens, try staying with it rather than turning away. This is you, too. Can you see yourself with compassion and acceptance?

Work with harder material. This exercise uses small flaws intentionally in order to help you strengthen your capacity for self-acceptance. As that capacity grows stronger, you might choose to start looking at more emotionally challenging aspects of yourself and your life—places of deeper and more abiding shame. We all have them. Find a good friend or a good therapist, and try telling that person the truth.

Further Reading: Books on Radical Acceptance

- Tara Brach, PhD, *Radical Acceptance: Embracing Your Life with the Heart of a Buddha*, Bantam Books, 2003.
- Anne Weiser Cornell, *The Radical Acceptance of Everything*, Calluna Press, 2005.

50

Ask

What's on your wish list? I'm not just talking about gifts and *stuff*. I'm talking about both your deepest desires and your most fleeting cravings. Write it all down, without any inhibition. Let yourself be as extravagant or grandiose or maniacal, as sentimental or dreamy or unrealistic as you feel. Perhaps what emerges will surprise you.

What You'll Need
- A pen
- Paper

How to Do It
1. **Empty your mind of desire.** Evolution has assured that desire is our mind's default mode. After all, when you don't know where your next meal is coming from, your mind adapts to filter all your perceptions through the lens of hunger. Desire sharpens our awareness of available resources and gives us an edge in acquiring

them. So start this exercise by taking a few slow breaths while trying to notice just your desiring mind at work. Do this by trying *not* to desire anything. How long does it take before desiring thoughts start crashing through? *I'm thirsty. I wonder what's for lunch. How long until this is over?* Take a minute or two just to notice these thoughts.

2. **Make your list.** What do you want? Pick up your pen and start writing. Start each sentence with the words "I want." As you do this, try to keep your pen moving, no matter what. If nothing comes to mind in a given moment, just write, "I want I want I want" until something pops into your head. Your thoughts may range from fulfilling immediate desires (*a hamburger*), to materialistic impulses (*an iPhone*), to grandiose fantasies (*untold wealth*), to deep emotional yearnings (*to be understood*). Write it all down without censoring anything that comes to mind, no matter how trivial or embarrassing it may seem. If it comes into your mind, some part of you wants it. Write until you feel like you can't possibly think of anything more.

3. **Keep making your list.** Now take a deep breath and write down all the things that you didn't let yourself write in step 2.

4. **Read your list.** Read it out loud and try to observe yourself as you do. Keep reading until something makes

you start to choke up. (If you're the stoic type, you'll just have to make an executive decision here: which item on your list has the largest emotional charge?)

5. **Ask.** When you've identified an emotionally charged desire (and there will almost certainly be more than one of them on your list, so feel free to repeat this step as often as you like), picture the person, entity, or force in your life that could potentially give it to you. It might be a spouse or a parent, it might the Universe, or it might be God. Calmly, out loud, in the simplest terms you can, make your request. Try to do this without anticipating any particular outcome, with awareness that the person or entity you are asking may or may not be able to give you what you want. Notice what you experience in your body and mind as you ask. Finally, destroy the paper (burning is good; shredding is okay, too), release your desire to the Universe, and get on with your life.

From Deprivation to Abundance

My father was born in 1929.

Sixty or so years later, I accompanied him on an overnight fishing trip. We had a motel room for the night, and we'd brought some food along with us—bread and sandwich meats, chips, granola, and a carton of milk. When we were packing up our things for the drive home, I picked up the half-filled milk carton and realized that it

was starting to turn sour. Without thinking, I started to pour it down the drain. My father stopped me with an edge of urgency in his voice.

"What are you doing?" he asked. "We should take that home."

"It's already going bad," I responded. "By the time we get home it will be totally rotten."

He paused, clearly struggling. It took him a long time to formulate his next sentence.

"When you grow up in the Depression," he said at last, "it's hard to throw away anything that you might possibly be able to use."

That sentence was a gift to me. I was suddenly able to understand so many of the confusing mixed messages about money and resources that had defined our family's life. No matter how financially secure the family was, beneath the surface we were always acting like we were in the Depression.

We all move through the present moment with expectations that we've carried forward from the past. Many (perhaps most) of us see the world as a place in which there are not (and will never be) enough resources to go around. If we see things this way, the consequences are many. We live a little more on edge, we tend to see our existence as a competitive struggle. And we tend to equate our receiving something with someone else being deprived of that same thing. Worse, we tend to get really moralistic about desire, hiding our own while shaming others for theirs. We live in a deprivation economy.

But what if it's not true? What if there's more than enough to go around? What if we can get what we need without depriving others? In fact, what if getting our needs met actually makes more resources available for others?

It's hard for many of us to imagine. But it's possible. Try it out. How would your world look from the perspective of an economy of abundance?

Variations: Giving and Receiving

Receive. If you are serious about asking for what you want, then you're also going to have to learn how to receive. I recommend that you start at the dinner table, with a simple and unemotional request: "Would you please pass the salt?" Consider what you're doing in this moment: you are briefly interrupting the flow of conversation and activity by placing your own personal need ahead of the group's. Notice what it feels like to ask, and more importantly, notice how it feels to have the salt passed to you. Can you identify tiny flashes of emotion (embarrassment, greediness, entitlement) in this most mundane of moments? Can you receive what you have asked for with grace and gratitude?

Say, "Thank you." It's good etiquette, of course, and if you're going to start asking for what you want,

you're also going to have to start learning to say it. But it's not always easy to say a clean, effective "thank you." Practice when you're alone, experimenting with the wide range of intonations that you can give the phrase. See if you can find a way of saying it in everyday situations that feels truly genuine without being so intense that it feels weird.

Say, "You're welcome." What do you say when you're at the checkout counter and the clerk hands you your receipt and says, "Thank you"? My guess is that you say "Thanks" right back. We all do. There's no harm in that, of course, but it always feels a little bit out of balance to me. We're both playing the role of giver; no one is taking the role of recipient. In situations like this, responding with "You're welcome" has actually come to feel a little strange. So practice saying this phrase out loud in a way that feels genuine and sincere. Then, the next time someone thanks you for something, let yourself be thanked. Say, "You're welcome." It's harder to do than you think.

Further Reading: Books on Abundance

- Laurence G. Boldt, *The Tao of Abundance: Eight Ancient Principles for Abundant Living*, Penguin/Arkana, 1999.
- Sarah Ban Breathnach, *Simple Abundance: A Daybook of Comfort and Joy*, Warner Books, 1995.
- John Randolph Price, *The Abundance Book*, Hay House, 2005.

51

Do Nothing

I won't lie to you. This is the hardest exercise in the book.

What You'll Need
• Nothing

How to Do It
1. **Do nothing.** Move gradually into this exercise. Start by doing nothing in particular. Precisely how you choose to do this is entirely up to you.
2. **Do nothing.** Deepen your practice by focusing on what is going on around you. But do nothing in response. Let it all happen. Be passive and refuse to react.
3. **Do nothing.** Now start to quiet your body. Find a comfortable position and hold as still as you can. Breathe if you must, but try to keep it to a minimum.
4. **Do nothing.** What's all that activity? It's your mind, racing around, doing things. Quiet your thoughts.

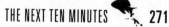

What's happening inside your body? You can feel your pulse; that's your blood chugging along. Your eyes blink. You look around. You subtly tense and relax different muscles. You swallow. Stay with it all. Keep noticing it. Keep trying to still all these activities.

5. **Do nothing.** Without choosing to do nothing, and without choosing not to do something, continue. Then when you are ready, get up and move on with your life.

Approximately Nothing

Recently, my eight-year-old son has taken to pointing out that it's impossible to do "nothing." He's very proud of having been able to figure this out, and he can go on in great detail about how many things you're actually doing when you seem to be doing "nothing."

He's right, of course. And you're right to wonder why in this exercise you've been sent off on such a fool's errand. What is the point?

I used to ask this same question when, as a child, I was told that I was supposed to try to be like Jesus, who, as I was also told, was "perfect."

It's not possible, I'd say.

Be as much like him as it is possible for you to be, was the response.

That answer used to rankle me so much. I felt like I was being set up. I could only fail. But in retrospect, I can

see a different sort of wisdom in attempting to emulate an ideal that is inherently unachievable.

Why try to do nothing?

Because trying, in and of itself, transforms our awareness. In the act of attempting to achieve a state of nothingness, we reveal to ourselves how many layers of "something" we are doing at any given moment. It brings us face-to-face with ourselves in the present moment. It brings us into reality.

And reality is a very good thing indeed.

Further Reading: Books About Nothing

- John D. Barrow, *The Book of Nothing: Vacuums, Voids, and the Latest Ideas about the Origins of the Universe*, Vintage Books, 2002.
- Frank Close, *Nothing: A Very Short Introduction*, Oxford University Press, 2009.
- Charles Seife, *Zero: The Biography of a Dangerous Idea*, Penguin, 2000.

Acknowledgments

I am grateful for the support of so many people, not just during the writing of this book but also during the years of contemplation, conversation, and training that led up to the writing.

To the faculty at the University of Montana Counselor Education program. To the masterful clinicians I've had the great fortune to study under during my postgraduate training: Dan Hughes, "the guys" (Glen, Kent, and Bert) from the Circle of Security Project, and Julie Larrieu. To my own therapists over the years, who have persistently pointed me in the general direction of reality. To my colleagues in Missoula, especially Melodee and Danette, who have seen me through it all. To my patients, who continue to expand my vision of what is possible. And most of all to Susanna, Ezekiel, and Otis, who guide me back to the simple power and beauty of the present moment, again and again and again.

Thank you.

Appendix A

How Are You Feeling?

This list will help you identify exercises you can use depending on how you're feeling right at this moment.

If You Are Feeling:	Try This Exercise:	If You Are Feeling:	Try This Exercise:
Aggressive	26. Pose a Threat	Angry	20. Give Thanks
			26. Pose a Threat
Agitated	13. Do Something		27. Hold Your Breath
	24. Pace		44. Dig in Your Heels
			45. Pout
Aimless	7. Take Baby Steps		
	11. Let Your Mind Wander	Anxious	2. Relax Your Face
			10. Catastrophize
Ambivalent	1. Procrastinate	Apathetic	14. Lust
	38. Decide		29. Levitate
Amorphous	34. Set Up a Perimeter	Ashamed	26. Pose a Threat
	35. Define Your Terms		49. Accept Reality
		At loose ends	19. Read the Instructions
			28. Feel Your Foot

Blank	13. Do Something	Deluded	10. Catastrophize
	51. Do Nothing		12. Lie to Yourself
			49. Accept Reality
Bored	9. Stare at the Wall		
	16. Misuse an Object	Deprived	18. Give It All Away
			20. Give Thanks
Burdened	1. Procrastinate		50. Ask
	4. Move as if You Are		
	Underwater	Detached	3. Go into Another
			Room
Bursting	23. Make a List		17. Retrieve an Item
	24. Pace		from the Trash
			28. Feel Your Foot
Childish	7. Take Baby Steps		42. Retrace Your Steps
	27. Hold Your Breath		43. Hear White Noise
	36. Plug Your Ears		51. Do Nothing
Confused	24. Pace	Disconnected	37. Write a Letter
	42. Retrace Your Steps		49. Accept Reality
Constrained	9. Stare at the Wall	Disorganized	11. Let Your Mind
	24. Pace		Wander
	25. Moan		23. Make a List
	41. Repeat Yourself		
		Disoriented	22. Get Lost
Craving	14. Lust		28. Feel Your Foot
	32. Wait		34. Set Up a Perimeter
	50. Ask		
		Distracted	4. Move as if You Are
Cynical	29. Levitate		Underwater
			11. Let Your Mind
Dangerous	26. Pose a Threat		Wander
	39. Surrender		40. Interrupt Yourself

Downtrodden	39. Surrender	Greedy	14. Lust
	48. Stand Up		17. Retrieve an Item from the Trash
Embarrassed	49. Accept Reality		18. Give It All Away
			50. Ask
Empty	51. Do Nothing		
		Guilty	10. Catastrophize
Excluded	33. Develop a Conspiracy Theory		39. Surrender
	34. Set Up a Perimeter	Harried	32. Wait
			40. Interrupt Yourself
Fearful	21. Hide		
	33. Develop a Conspiracy Theory	Histrionic	8. Animate a Memory
			26. Pose a Threat
			41. Repeat Yourself
Flawed	10. Catastrophize		
	49. Accept Reality	Hopeless	23. Make a List
			29. Levitate
Flighty	28. Feel Your Foot		39. Surrender
	29. Levitate		
		Hungry	14. Lust
Forgetful	5. Memorize a Data Sequence		32. Wait
	30. Look Around	Hyperactive	4. Move as if You Are Underwater
	47. Dwell in the Past		13. Do Something
			40. Interrupt Yourself
Fragmented	23. Make a List		
	40. Interrupt Yourself	Idealistic	10. Catastrophize
			19. Read the Instructions
Frustrated	24. Pace		49. Accept Reality
	40. Interrupt Yourself		
		Immobile	7. Take Baby Steps
Grandiose	24. Pace		13. Do Something
	33. Develop a Conspiracy Theory		48. Stand Up

Impatient	24. Pace		Inert	7. Take Baby Steps
	32. Wait			13. Do Something
				38. Decide
Imprisoned	9. Stare at the Wall			
	34. Set Up a Perimeter		Inflexible	1. Procrastinate
	39. Surrender			27. Hold Your Breath
				44. Dig in Your Heels
Impulsive	26. Pose a Threat			
	27. Hold Your Breath		Inhibited	14. Lust
				34. Set Up a Perimeter
In a rut	3. Go into Another Room			41. Repeat Yourself
	11. Let Your Mind Wander		Invaded	3. Go into Another Room
	16. Misuse an Object			34. Set Up a Perimeter
In denial	12. Lie to Yourself		Irritable	20. Give Thanks
	36. Plug Your Ears			40. Interrupt Yourself
	49. Accept Reality			
			Lifeless	8. Animate a Memory
In pain	25. Moan			27. Hold Your Breath
Inarticulate	35. Define Your Terms		Listless	8. Animate a Memory
	46. Speak			35. Define Your Terms
Incompetent	16. Misuse an Object		Lost	3. Go into Another Room
	19. Read the Instructions			21. Hide
				22. Get Lost
Indecisive	13. Do Something			30. Look Around
	38. Decide			37. Write a Letter
Ineffective	19. Read the Instructions		Manipulative	12. Lie to Yourself
	23. Make a List			26. Pose a Threat
				45. Pout

Mischievous	21. Hide	Overconfident	10. Catastrophize
			33. Develop a
Needy	18. Give It All Away		Conspiracy Theory
	24. Pace		39. Surrender
	50. Ask		
		Over-	31. Power Down
Numb	28. Feel Your Foot	stimulated	36. Plug Your Ears
	43. Hear White Noise		43. Hear White Noise
Oblivious	6. Throw Something	Over-	1. Procrastinate
	Away	whelmed	31. Power Down
	22. Get Lost		36. Plug Your Ears
	30. Look Around		43. Hear White Noise
			51. Do Nothing
Obstinate	1. Procrastinate		
	44. Dig in Your Heels	Panicky	10. Catastrophize
	51. Do Nothing		21. Hide
			34. Set Up a Perimeter
On automatic	3. Go into Another		
pilot	Room	Pessimistic	12. Lie to Yourself
	13. Do Something		20. Give Thanks
	42. Retrace Your Steps		23. Make a List
Oppressed	34. Set Up a Perimeter	Porous	34. Set Up a Perimeter
	39. Surrender		
	45. Pout	Powerless	26. Pose a Threat
			39. Surrender
Out of control	4. Move as if You Are		49. Accept Reality
	Underwater		
	14. Lust	Resentful	27. Hold Your Breath
	38. Decide		36. Plug Your Ears
	51. Do Nothing		45. Pout
Out of touch	22. Get Lost	Resistant	1. Procrastinate
	37. Write a Letter		44. Dig in Your Heels
	47. Dwell in the Past		

Restless	4. Move as if You Are Underwater	Sullen	45. Pout
	13. Do Something	Tense	2. Relax Your Face
			28. Feel Your Foot
Sadistic	20. Give Thanks		
	26. Pose a Threat	Thirsty	15. Have a Drink
Scared	10. Catastrophize	Tired	31. Power Down
	21. Hide		51. Do Nothing
	22. Get Lost		
		Tongue-tied	40. Interrupt Yourself
Self-conscious	2. Relax Your Face		41. Repeat Yourself
	41. Repeat Yourself		46. Speak
	42. Retrace Your Steps		
		Trapped	9. Stare at the Wall
Sneaky	21. Hide		34. Set Up a Perimeter
Stressed out	1. Procrastinate	Unbalanced	7. Take Baby Steps
	4. Move as if You Are Underwater		48. Stand Up
	28. Feel Your Foot	Uncertain	30. Look Around
			34. Set Up a Perimeter
Stubborn	1. Procrastinate		38. Decide
	27. Hold Your Breath		
	41. Repeat Yourself	Unfocused	5. Memorize a Data Sequence
	44. Dig in Your Heels		23. Make a List
			41. Repeat Yourself
Stuck	1. Procrastinate		
	8. Animate a Memory	Unfulfilled	14. Lust
	23. Make a List		18. Give It All Away
	24. Pace		50. Ask
	41. Repeat Yourself		
	44. Dig in Your Heels	Ungrounded	28. Feel Your Foot
	47. Dwell in the Past		47. Dwell in the Past

Appendix B

How Would You Like to Feel?

Like appendix A, this list outlines the correspondence between the exercises in this book and specific states of mind. In this case, however, you start by identifying a target state—how you'd like to feel; then you can identify the exercises that will move you in that direction.

If You'd Like to Feel a Sense of:	Try This Exercise:	If You'd Like to Feel a Sense of:	Try This Exercise:
Abundance	14. Lust	Clarity	21. Hide
	18. Give It all Away		30. Look Around
	50. Ask		38. Decide
			50. Ask
Acceptance	6. Throw Something Away		
	16. Misuse an Object	Comfort	10. Catastrophize
	18. Give It All Away		21. Hide
	39. Surrender		31. Power Down
	49. Accept Reality		
		Compassion	47. Dwell in the Past
Change	3. Go into Another Room		49. Accept Reality
	11. Let Your Mind Wander	Connection	2. Relax Your Face
	13. Do Something		17. Retrieve an Item from the Trash
	16. Misuse an Object		27. Hold Your Breath
	41. Repeat Yourself		37. Write a Letter

Hope	12. Lie to Yourself	Optimism	12. Lie to Yourself
	13. Do Something		23. Make a List
	29. Levitate		26. Pose a Threat
	39. Surrender		39. Surrender
	50. Ask		50. Ask
Integration	7. Take Baby Steps	Peace	2. Relax Your Face
	25. Moan		10. Catastrophize
	28. Feel Your Foot		21. Hide
	40. Interrupt Yourself		26. Pose a Threat
	43. Hear White Noise		31. Power Down
			36. Plug Your Ears
Intensity	14. Lust		51. Do Nothing
	32. Wait		
	45. Pout	Potential	3. Go into Another Room
			11. Let Your Mind Wander
Liberation	9. Stare at the Wall		12. Lie to Yourself
	18. Give It All Away		16. Misuse an Object
	22. Get Lost		
	39. Surrender	Power	26. Pose a Threat
			27. Hold Your Breath
Momentum	1. Procrastinate		29. Levitate
	7. Take Baby Steps		33. Develop a Conspiracy Theory
	13. Do Something		40. Interrupt Yourself
	14. Lust		45. Pout
	24. Pace		
	44. Dig in Your Heels	Purpose	4. Move as if You Are Underwater
	47. Dwell in the Past		5. Memorize a Data Sequence
Non-attachment	6. Throw Something Away		17. Retrieve an Item from the Trash
	16. Misuse an Object		38. Decide
	18. Give It All Away